The
Smith and Kraus
Play Index for
Young Actors Grades 6–12

Edited by
Craig Slaight,
Jennifer Esty, and
Elizabeth E. Monteleone

San Jose, CA 95129

YOUNG ACTORS SERIES

A Smith and Kraus Book

A Smith and Kraus Book
Published by Smith and Kraus, Inc.
PO Box 127, Lyme, NH 03768
www.SmithKraus.com

Copyright ©1999 by Smith and Kraus
All rights reserved
Manufactured in the United States of America
Cover and Text Design by Julia Hill Gignoux

First Edition: December 1999
10 9 8 7 6 5 4 3 2 1

The Library of Congress Cataloging-In-Publication Data
The Smith and Kraus young actor index. —1st ed.
p. cm. — (Young actors series)

Summary: An index of over 500 plays for middle and high school students as well as a plot summary and information for each play including author, style, cast size, and leasing agent.

ISBN 1-57525-050-0

1. Drama—Indexes—Juvenile literature.
2. Drama—Stories, plots, etc.—Juvenile literature.
[1. Drama—Indexes. 2. Drama—Stories, plots, etc.]
I. Series: Young actor series.

Z5781.S67   1998
[PN1655]
016.80882—dc21   98-10590
CIP
AC

Contents

The Teacher As Artistic Director

If there is one thing one learns very early on when setting out to direct Youth Theater it is that *"The Play's the Thing!"* Consider the typical scenario. You accept the job of directing a play with young actors, to be presented to a public audience. You shake the hand of the principal, the head of school, the department chair, or the local youth theatre producer, confident that you've been trained with depth and insight into the many facets of the theater, you've experienced the highs and lows of many productions on your own, and you've made a particular commitment to the theater journey of the young. Before the ink is set on your contract, you just know the question is going to be asked, *"What play are you going to do?"* And although you were prepared for that inevitable question, it still rings in your ears and strikes just a bit of fear in the deepest part of your being

It is the rare engagement that comes attached with the play already chosen. When the play HAS been chosen and you are brought in as director, the experience is usually less than rewarding. Why is that? I propose that the answer lies in our belief system. We are artists as well as teachers and so what we believe in is essential to what we produce. If you've spent any time at all directing or producing Youth Theater you will agree that the series of compromises (our constant brick wall) begins from the moment we consider *"What play are you going to do?"*

Sitting not too far from your favorite reading chair is a stack of weathered well-worn play catalogues. Since the quest to find plays to produce is endless, we all pour over these catalogues over and over again in the hopes of finding that gem—the one play that got by last time we folded the pages—the one that is sure to be a hit with our young actors and our audience. As "Compromise" spots you in your chair, digging deeply for the perfect play, already his essence is washing over you. Page after page of plays meets your eyes—each more un-perfect than the last. You know the pangs of recognition: *not enough women; requires far to complicated a set; themes are too mature for my principal; not enough women; oh!*

Perfect!—No I've already done that one; too many men; recommended for "mature" audiences (the same thing as—there goes my job) and on and on and on. Before spending another season in that reading chair, folding over the pages of this year's catalogue, stop—breathe—and consider another route.

I work for a major American regional theater that just so happens to have a large education program. Yes, the powers to be here are kind, and benevolent, and supportive. But I still have to answer the question "What play are you going to do?" And I, too, have my reading chair, and all of the current catalogues. Over the years, however, I've taken time to watch the workings of this major regional theater, and particularly the role of the Artistic Director. Boy oh boy, talk about someone who has to answer the question "What play are you going to do"! A few years ago it began to dawn on me. The Artistic Director's job was a lot like my job. We both had an audience that demanded our best, we both answered to a higher authority, we both had a company of actors (granted mine were far less accomplished, but a company nonetheless), and we both had to pick plays to produce with that company for that audience. That moment of recognition was rather like having an epiphany—*I was an Artistic Director too!* On that day, I turned the corner about how I picked my plays to produce with young people.

Once I started to think like an artistic director, I really began to challenge my beliefs; not just my beliefs about life, although it begins there, but my beliefs about what I was teaching and about the role of theater in the lives of those I was charged with leading. I not only had to think of "what play?" but I suddenly felt that I had to consider "why theater?" I took myself on my own artistic retreat and contemplated the "why" of my work. This included assessing my own artistic needs—I am not just a teacher, I am an *artist-educator.* What I needed to say as an artist was as essential as what my students needed to learn and what challenges my audiences needed to face. I also assessed my "company." I took stock of just where my actors were in their training—their abilities—their potential. I couldn't very well produce a play that I was on fire about if the actors weren't up for the demands of the play. Where were they? Where did I want them to go? Where was I? Where did I want to go? Finally, I took stock in my audience. What had they seen? How did I want to challenge them? Where could we go together as theatre artists and audience, communicating back and forth across the edge of the stage? This gave my whole play selection process new juice—and I'm convinced that *juice* is key to passion and growth. In India, it's called Rasa. I needed Rasa in my program and I needed to start thinking of the "why" of my choices before going one-step further.

When my self-assessment was complete, I began to look for plays that did what I wanted them to do. In some cases this meant that I had to seek writers to write new plays, which has led me to a whole new phase of my work, commissioning new plays. But what essentially remains is that I look for work that challenges me, my actors, and my audience—and not just something that will "fill the bill."

My publishers, Smith and Kraus, were very involved with the juice of youth theater, having committed themselves to many years of producing numerous volumes of monologues, scenes, and complete plays that specifically address the young actors' world. They joined us in our quest for finding plays suitable to produce with young people. What is before you is the result of a number of years of rigorous digging into stacks and stacks of available plays (and some that are not so available) to glean a workable digest for your use in answering the question, "What play are you going to do?"

This digest is a guide, not an end to your quest. We recognize that you may well have produced what you feel is the perfect play and that play isn't listed here. We recognize that this guide is only suitable if it meets your goals. We recognize that your particular requirements are just that, *particular,* and that the uniqueness of theater, actors, audience, is what makes it so interesting and so frustrating. But we do hope that what is here is an intelligent beginning—a synthesis of many sources to one that fits in your hand, one that you can mark up and bend the pages to suit your goals.

There are a few things that you need to know about how to use this guide.

1. The plays detailed within are selected for use with young actors grades 6 through 12. There is much room for diversity in that age range, and it would be wrong to misread our intentions by saying that every entry will be suitable for every situation. Some schools are only beginning to

train young actors. Other programs have spent years developing a highly sophisticated group of actors and an audience to meet their challenges. You must be guided by your goals and the dynamics of your program.

2. If you wish to produce a play from this digest you must secure permission for such a production. The copyright and performance laws are strict and very specific. In many cases it doesn't matter if you are charging admission or not, you must first secure the rights to perform— which often requires the payment of a royalty. Please consult the appropriate representative for the property, which is identified in the listing at the end of the book.

3. Please understand that playwrights often move from agency to agency and that new companies can represent their properties. The representation of the plays listed are as they appeared at the time of publication. If you cannot find the playwright's representative, you can try contacting the Dramatists Guild for updated information (212-398-9366).

4. Any property listed as "Public Domain" (PD) does not require permission or royalty payment. However, some plays exist in translation or adaptation, and those translations and adaptations are subject to the same legal permissions as the original property. Please check closely when looking into a work that has been adapted or translated.

5. For the purposes of this digest one-act plays normally run between twenty and thirty minutes and "short plays" may run up to an hour.

Finally, I applaud your rigor and discipline in seeking the most stimulating plays to produce with your young actors. We share a common quest with very specific requirements. We are tested daily and we all work valiantly to stave off compromise. I hope this guide will help buffer the blows and aid you in your ongoing mission.

Craig Slaight
San Francisco
October, 1999

Play
Information
Index

TITLE	AUTHOR
100 Lunches	Jack Sharkey & Leo W. Sears
1940s Radio Hour, The	Walton Jones
Abe Lincoln for the Defense	L.E. McCullough
Abie's Irish Rose	Anne Nichols
Adventures of Huckleberry Finn	Randal Myler
Adventures of Tom Sawyer, The	Timothy Mason
African Company Presents Richard III, The	Carlyle Brown
African Tales: Kalulu and His Money Farm and Rumpelstiltskin	Timothy Mason
Afternoon of the Elves	Y. York
Ah Wilderness!	Eugene O'Neill
Aladdin and the Wonderful Lamp	Timothy Mason
Album	David Rimmer
All's Well That Ends Well	William Shakespeare
Almost an Eagle	Michael Kimberly
American Dame, The	Philip C. Lewis
American Primitive or John and Abigail	William Gibson
Amulets Against the Dragon Forces	Paul Zindel
Analiese	Lynne Alvarez
Anastasia	Guy Bolton
Anastasia File, The	Royce Ryton
And Never Been Kissed	Aurand Harris
…and stuff…	Peter Dee
…And the Rain Came to Mayfield	Jason Milligan
And They Dance Real Slow In Jackson	Jim Leonard, Jr.
Andromache	Euripides
Animal Farm	adapted by Nelson Bond
Anna K	Eugenie Leontovich
Anne of Green Gables	L. M. Montgomery
Another Country	Julian Mitchell
Antic Spring	Robert Nail

STYLE	CAST	LEASING
comedy	3m 3f	SF
musical	10m 5f	SF
one-act	18m 4f	S&K
comedy	6m 2f	SF
comedy	10m 4f	Dramatic
short play	30 mixed cast	ICM
drama	5m 2f	DPS
short play	11 m&f	ICM
drama	1m 5f	Dramatic
comedy	9m 6f	SF
short play	30 mixed cast	ICM
comedy	2m 2f	DPS
comedy	10m 4f	public domain
comedy	5m	SF
comedy (play out)	2m 3f	DPS
history	4m 4f	DPS
drama	9m 3f	DPS
drama	8m 8f flexible	JKA
drama	8m 5f	SF
drama	2m 2f	SF
comedy	5m 7f	SF
comedy	flexible	SF
drama	6m 3f	SF
drama	3m 4f	DPS
tragedy	4m 5f	public domain
reading	5m 2f	SF
drama	6m 5f	SF
musical	12m 17f	SF
drama	10, flexible	SF
one-act comedy	3m 3f	SF

STYLE	CAST	LEASING
tragedy	3m 3f 10, chorus	public domain
poetic fantasy	4m 1f	SF
comedy	11m 3f	DPS
comedy	16m 5f	public domain
comedy	4m 5f	DPS
drama	6m 4f	Dramatic
play	2m 3f	DPS
comedy	3m 3f	SF
musical	14m 17f	SF
musical	11m 8f	TW
romantic comedy	12m 5f	DPS
short play	8m 6f	ICM
drama	5m 5f	SF
drama	13m 9w	Dramatic
drama	2m 2f	SF
x-mas comedy	12m 15f	SF
comedy	4m	SF
short play	1m, one box	SF
drama	10m 10f. flexible	DPS
comedy	3m 5f	SF
drama	4m 4f, chorus	Gersh
drama	3m 4f	S&K
drama	3m 3f	SF
play from Gospels	min. 24	DPS
comedy/mystery/thriller	5m 8f (flexible)	SF
drama	4m 3f	SF
comedy	7m 2f	DPS
play	2m 4f	DPS
drama	3m 4f	SF

TITLE	AUTHOR
Bride of Brachenloch! The	Rick Abbot
Brighton Beach Memoirs	Neil Simon
Broken Rainbows	Mary Hall Surface
Brother Goose	William Davidson
Bullshot Crummond	Ron House
Bye Bye Birdie	Stewart/Strouse/Adams
By Hex	John Renier, Howard Blankman, & Richard Gehman
Caesar and Cleopatra	Bernard Shaw
Cage, The	Mario Fratie
Caine Mutiny Court-Martial, The	Herman Wouk
Camille	Alexandre Dumas trans. Henriette Metcalf
Can't Buy Me Love	Jason Milligan
Carousel	Rodgers/ Hammerstein
Catch 22	Joseph Heller
Catholic School Girls	Casey Kurtti
Cat's Paw	William Mastosimone
Cermonies in Dark Old Men	Lonne Elder
Chat Botté (Puss in Boots)	Pamela Gerke
Cheaper by the Dozen	Christopher Sergel adapted from Frank Gilbreth & Ernestine Gilbreth Carey
Cherry Orchard, The	Anton Chekhov
Children of a Lesser God	Mark Medoff
Children's Hour, The	Lillian Hellman
Choices	Walden Theatre Young Playwrights
Chopin Playoffs, The	Israel Horovitz
Class Action	Brad Slaight
Class Dismissed	Craig J. Nevius

STYLE	CAST	LEASING
Gothic thriller	3m 8f	SF
comedy/drama	3m 4f	SF
drama	2m 2f	S&K
comedy	3m 9f	Dramatic
farce	3m 2f	SF
musical	22m 26f	TW
musical	9m 5f	DPS
comedy	20m 5f	SF
drama	5m 3f	SF
drama	19m	SF
drama	11m 6f	SF
one-act comedy	3f	SF
musical	12m 7f	RHML
comedy	9-36m 2-8f	SF
comedy	4f	SF
drama	2m 2f	SF
drama, Black Groups	5m 2f	SF
one-act	min 7 / max 25 m&f	S&K
comedy	9m 7f	Dramatic
drama	9m 5f	DPS
drama	3m 4f	DPS
drama	2m 12f	DPS
comedy/drama (scenes and monos)	10-20	Dramatic
comedy	5m 3f	DPS
collected	3m 4f	Baker's
comic drama	13m 12f	SF

TITLE	AUTHOR
Cleveland	Mac Welman
Club, The	Eve Merriam
Cockeyed Kite	Joseph Caldwell
Colored Museum, The	Wolfe
Colored People's Time	Leslie Lee
Come Slowly, Eden	Norman Rosten
Comedy of Errors	William Shakespeare
Competition Piece	John Wells
Contrast, The	Royall Tyler
Courtship	Horton Foote
Cowardy Custard	Noel Coward
Cradle Song, The	G. Martinez-Sierra, trans. John Garrett Underhill
Crucible, The	Arthur Miller
Cry Havoc	Allan Kenward
Culabra, La (The Snake)	Pamela Gerke
Curious Savage, The	John Patrick
Da-Hoos-Whee-Whee	Pamela Gerke
Daddy Long Legs	Jean Webster
Daddy's Home	Ivan Menchall
Dags	Debra Oswald
Dames at Sea	George Haimsohn/ Robin Miller/Jim Wise
Dance and the Railroad, The	David Henry Hwang
Dancers, The	Horton Foote
Dancing Feathers	Kleitsch and Stephens
Dancing Solo	Mary Hall Surface
Dancing with Strangers	Sandra Fenichel Asher
Dark of the Moon	Howard Richardson & William Berney
Daughter of a Traveling Lady	Peter Dee

STYLE	CAST	LEASING
short play	3m 7f	ICM
musical	flexible	SF
drama	8m 5f	DPS
drama	2m, 4f	GA
Black history	6m 3f	SF
drama	5m 2f	DPS
comedy	11m 5f	public domain
one-act comedy	10-21, various	SF
comedy	5m 4f	SF
drama	3m 5f	DPS
revue	6m 6f	SF
romantic	4m 10f	SF
drama	10m 10f	DPS
drama	13f	SF
one-act	min 5 / max 25 m&f	S&K
comedy	5m 6f	DPS
one-act	min 10 / max 35 m&f	S&K
comedy	6m 7f	SF
one-act drama	1m 1f	SF
comedy	4m 6f	Dramatic
musical comedy	4m 3f	SF
one-act drama	2m	DPS
one-act drama	3m 7f	DPS
drama		Annick
drama	2m 3f	Dramatic
trilogy of short plays	3m 6f	Dramatic
drama	28 roles	SF
one-act comedy-drama	1m 2f	SF

TITLE	AUTHOR
David and Lisa	Theodore Isaac Reach adapt. James Rubin
¿De Dónde?	Mary Gallagher
Dear Ruth	Norman Krasna
Death in Scarsdale	Victor Levin
Death Takes a Holiday	Alberto Cassella
Deep Blue Funk and Other Stories	Daniel B. Frank and Arnold Aprill
Design for Murder	George Baston
Diamonds	collaborative
Diary of Anne Frank, The	Frances Goodrich and Albert Hackett
Dining Room, The	A. R. Gurney
Dino	Rose, Reginald
Disappearance of the Jews, The	David Mamet
Dispute, La	Marivaux, trans. Timberlake Wertenbaker
Diviners, The	James Leonard
Do You See What I'm Saying?	Megan Terry
Does a Tiger Wear a Necktie?	Don Peterson
Doll's House, A	Henrik Ibsen
Doll's House, A	Henrik Ibsen adapted by Albert Pia
Don Juan	Molière trans. Albert Bermel
Don't Count On Forever	Nancy Pahl Gilsenan
Don't Drink the Water	Woody Allen
Dorothy Meets Alice	Joseph Robinette
Down from the Sky	Geraldine Ann Snyder & Paul Lenzi
Dracula	Christopher Nichols
Dreamtime Down Under	L.E. McCullough

STYLE	CAST	LEASING
drama	11m 11f	SF
drama	8m 5f	DPS
comedy	5m 5f	DPS
one-act comedy	3m 2f	Dramatic
drama	7m 6f	SF
one-act drama	1m 4f	Dramatic
Thriller	4m 6f	SF
musical revue	7m 3f	SF
drama	5m 5f	DPS
play	3m 3f	DPS
drama	8m 10f	Dramatic
one-act drama	2m	SF
comedy	mix	Dramatic
drama	6m 5f	SF
drama	7f	SF
drama/comedy	14m, 3f	DPS
drama	3m 4f	SF
one-act drama	3m 3f	Dramatic
satirical drama	18-20m 3-4f	SF
drama	6m 8f	Dramatic
comedy	12m 4f	SF
musical	11, flexible	Dramatic
musical	3m 2f	Dramatic
one-act thriller	5m 1f or 2m 4f	Dramatic
one-act	4m 2f	S&K

TITLE	AUTHOR
Dutchman	Baraka (formerly LeRoi Jones)
Dybbuk, The	S. Ansky
East of the Sun, West of the Moon	Pamela Gerke
Echoes	Vaughn McBride
Eddie "Mundo" Edmundo	Lynne Alvarez
Educating Rita	Willy Russell
Effect of Gamma Rays, The	Paul Zindel
Electra	Euripedes
Encounter 500	Mario Fratti & Guiseppi Murolo
Endangered Species, An	Kathy Sorenson
Enemy of the People	Henrik Ibsen
Enter Laughing	Joseph Stein
Equus	Peter Shaffer
Every 17 Minutes the Crowd Goes Crazy!	Paul Zindel
Everyman/ Everywoman	Virginia Egermeir
Faith County	Mark Landon Smith
Fame	David De Silva from Christopher Gore
Family Devotions	David Henry Hwang
Fantastiks	Schmidt/Jones
Father, The	August Strindberg, trans. John Osborne & Harry G. Carlson
Feng Zhen-Zhu (The Wind Pearl)	Pamela Gerke
Fiddler on the Roof	Harnick/Stein/Brock
Fionn in Search of His Youth	L.E. McCullough
First Breeze of Summer, The	Lee
First Impressions	Abe Burrow's adapt. from Austen

STYLE	CAST	LEASING
drama	2m 1f	SF
drama	24m, 7f	SF
one-act	min 7 / max 50 m&f	S&K
evening of monologues	variable	Dramatic
drama	3m 3f	JKA
drama	1m 1f	SF
drama	5f	DPS
tragedy	5m 2f	public domain
musical	8m 4f	SF
drama	3m 4f	SF
drama	10m 3s	S&K
comedy	7m 4f	SF
morality drama	5m 4f	SF
drama	8m 6f	DPS
modern allegory	4m 5f, 6-10 either	Dramatic
comedy	3m 6f	SF
drama	9m 15w	Dramatic
drama	4m 5f	DPS
musical	7m 1f	MT1
drama	5m 3f	SF
one-act	min 12 / max 40 m&F	S&K
musical	12m 10f	MT1
one-act	5m 2f	S&K
drama (Black groups)	8m 6f	SF
musical comedy	14m 12f	SF

STYLE	CAST	LEASING
musical	48m 12f	SF
one-act	8m 6f	S&K
farce	6m 2f	SF
one-act	11m 2f	S&K
comedy	2m 1f	DPS
comedy	7m 7f	SF
comedy	5m 2f	DPS
drama	4m 4f	SF
one-act	4m 4f	S&K
drama	4m 5f	DPS
bio	27m 4f	SF
comedy	6m 10f	Dramatic
Christmas drama	2m 5f	Dramatic
one-act	7m 3f	S&K
comedy	2f	SF
comedy	3f	SF
monologue collection	5f	SF
documentary drama	14m 6f	SF
drama	8m 15f	Dramatic
comedy	5m 3f	SF
musical	5m 5f	TMax
musical comedy	5m 3f	SF
comedy	2m 3f	SF
comedy	3m 7f or 4m 6f	SF
comedy	20m 8f	DPS
musical	9m 8f	SF

STYLE	CAST	LEASING
drama	7m 8f	SF
musical comedy	8m 8f	DPS
comedy	2m	SF
one-act comedy/drama	3m 4f	SF
one-act	7m 4f	S&K
drama	6m 3f	DPS
musical	12m 11f flexible chorus	Dramatic
farce	7m 6f	SF
one-act comedy	3m 3f	DPS
drama	2m 2f	SF
comedy	6m 4f	SF
drama	6m 7f & 3 extras	Dramatic
one-act comedy/drama	3m 3f	Bakers
"an entertainment"	3m 1f	SF
musical	8m 6f	SF
drama	10f, extras	SF
drama	5m 2f	SF
one-act musical	6-30 mix	SF
one-act	14 chorus	S&K
folk opera	12m 10f	SF
comedy	3m 3f	DPS
drama	4m 7f	Dramatic
one-act comedy	4m 4f	Dramatic
drama	6m 6f	Dramatic

STYLE	CAST	LEASING
drama	9m 6f	DPS
drama	7m, 2f	ICM
drama (scenes and monos)	variable	Dramatic
drama	23m 7f	DPS
one-act drama	2m 2f	SF
melodrama	1m 3f 1boy 1 girl	SF
drama	3m 4f	SF
one-act drama	3m 2f	SF
drama	3m 3f (more possible)	Dramatic
fantasy	4m 3f	SF
drama	4m 6f	U of C
comedy	7m 13f	Dramatic
comedy	26m 17f	SF
drama	10m 12f	SF
comedy	4m 10f	DPS
drama	6m, 5f	SF
dramatic reading	3 speaking parts, chorus	DPS
one-act	10m 8f	S&K
history	13m 2f	Dramatic
one-act drama	1m 2f	Dramatic
one-act drama	7m (f)	Dramatic
short play	11m 2 f	ICM
one-act	4m 2f	S&K
musical farce	6m 2f	SF
drama	5f	SF
comedy	8m 3f	DPS
tragedy	19m 7f	DPS

STYLE	CAST	LEASING
drama	10m 12f	Dramatic
one-act comedy	3f	DPS
comedy	4m 6f	SF
one-act	min 11 / max 30 m&f	S&K
play	4m 3f	DPS
drama	4m 4f	WM
comedy	2m 3f	SF
comedy	3m	SF
comedy	2m 25f	DPS
play	4m 3f	DPS
musical melodrama	4m 4f	Dramatic
musical comedy	5m 4f	SF
comedy	5m 7f	SF
one-act comedy	3m	DPS
one-act drama	8m 5f	Dramatic
comedy/drama	flexible	Dramatic
drama	1m 1f	author
comedy	3m 5f	Dramatic
drama	12m 5f	SF
drama	8m, 3f	H&W
play	4m 3f	DPS
musical	10m 5f	SF
thriller	3m 5f	DPS
drama	1m 3f	SF
comedy	10m 13f	SF
drama	1m	Bantam
drama	18m 3f	SF

TITLE	AUTHOR
Man Who Lost the River, The	Bernard Sabath
Mandrake	Machiavelli, trans. Frederick May & Eric Bentley
Marcus Brutus	Paul Foster
Mask, The	Dorothy R. Murphree
Master Harold...and the Boys	Athol Fugard
Mataora and Niwareka in the Underworld	Pamela Gerke
Matchmaker, The	Thorton Wilder
Matsuyama Mirror, The	Velina Hasu Houston
Me and My Girl	L. Arthur Rose/Douglas Furber/Noel Gay
Me Nobody Knows, The	Robert Livingston & Herb Schapiro
Medea	Euripides
Merrily We Roll Along	Sondheim/Furth
Midnight Caller, The	Horton Foote
Midsummer Night's Dream, A	William Shakespeare
Mikado, The	Gilbert & Sullivan
Minnie's Boys	Arthur Marx & Robert Fisher
Minuet, A	Louis N. Parker
Miracle Worker, The	William Gibson
Miss Firecracker Contest, The	Beth Henley
Mister Magister	Thomas F. Monteleone
Mixed Babies	Oni Faida Lampley
Moby Dick Rehearsed	Orson Welles, from Herman Melville
Monkey King, The	L.E. McCullough
Monkey's Paw, The	W. W. Jacobs & Louis N. Parker
Moon over the Brewery	Bruce Graham
Most Dangerous Woman in Amer., The	L.E. McCullough

STYLE	CAST	LEASING
comedy/drama	5m 5f	Dramatic
drama	5m 5f	SF
dramatic tragedy	9m 4f	SF
one-act drama	2m 2f	Dramatic
drama	3m (1 white, 2 black)	SF
one-act	min 8 / max 25 m&f	S&K
comedy	9m 7f	SF
one-act	1m 8f	H&CA
musical	11m 8f	SF
musical	12 total	SF
tragedy	5m 2f	public domain
musical	27 mix	SF
one-act drama	2m 5f	DPS
comedy	13m 7f	public domain
musical	flexible	SF
musical	1f mix	SF
one-act poetic drama	2m 1f	SF
drama	7m 7f	SF
comedy	2m 4f	DPS
one-act drama	5m, 1f	WM
drama	5f	DPS
melodrama	12m 2f	SF
one-act	3m 2f chorus	S&K
one-act thriller	4m 1f	SF
drama	2m 2f	DPS
one-act	7m 7f	S&K

TITLE	AUTHOR
Most Valuable Player	Mary Hall Surface
Mother Hicks	Susan L. Zeder
Mothers and Daughters	Mario Fratti
Mr. Scrooge	Richard Morris, Dolores Claman & Ted Wood
Ms. Scrooge	P. M. Clepper
Murder Takes the Veil	Margaret Ann
Museum	Tina Howe
Musical Comedy Murders of 1940	John Bishop
My Children! My Africa!	Athol Fugard
My Sister Eileen	Joseph Fields & Jerome Chodorov
My Sister in This House	Wendy Kesselman
Mystery of Irma Vep, The	Charles Ludlam
Ne Holmolaiset (The Silly Villagers)	Pamela Gerke
Nerd, The	Larry Shue
Never Mind What Happened, How Did It End?	David Rogers
Nice People Dancing To Good Country Music	Lee Blessing
Nightingale, The	Timothy Mason
Nights in Hohokus	Jason Milligan
No Exit	Jean Paul Sartre
No Place to Be Somebody	Charles Gordone
Noah	Andre Obey
Noises Off	Michael Frayn
Nutcracker, The	June Walker Rogers
Of Poems, Youth and Spring	John Logan
Oklahoma	Rodgers/Hammerstein
Oliver	Bart
Once a Catholic	Mary O'Malley

STYLE	CAST	LEASING
drama	12m 5f	CTC
drama	1m 2f chorus	Dramatic
mystery	2m 4f	SF
Christmas musical	10m 9f, 4 ghosts, extras	Dramatic
Christmas	22f	Dramatic
mystery	8m 15f	Dramatic
comedy	9m 9f	SF
comedy	5m 5f	DPS
drama	2m 1f	SF
comedy	21m 6f	DPS
drama	4f	SF
comedy	2m	SF
one-act	min 7 / max 25 m&f	S&K
comedy	5m 2f	DPS
comedy	19m 19f (doubling possible)	Dramatic
play	3m 2f	DPS
short play	3m 3 f 6 mixed cast	ICM
one-act comedy	2m	SF
drama	2m 2f	SF
drama	11m 5f	SF
fantasy	5m 4f	SF
farce	5m 4f	SF
Christmas fantasy	10m 12f	Dramatic
one-act comedy	1m 1f (3 voices, 4 chorus)	SF
musical	1f. mixed	RHML
musical	1m mixed	TW
comedy	4m 10f	SF

STYLE	CAST	LEASING
comedy	24m 14f	SF
musical	1m mixed	RHML
one-act comedy	1m 1f	Dramatic
fairy tale	17m 11f	SF
comedy/drama	13m 4f	SF
short play	2m 1f	author
drama	6m 3f	Dramatic
comic drama	3m	SF
comedy	5m 12f	Dramatic
drama	17m 7f	SF
drama	1m 1f	DPS
drama	10m 8f	Dramatic
one-act play of ideas	4m 2f	SF
one-act drama	2m 1f	author
poetic fantasy	26m 12f	SF
drama	5m 3f	DPS
thriller	1f 4m	SF
fantasy	25, mix	SF
musical	6m 4f, flexible chorus	Dramatic
comedy	9m 6f	SF
mystery	8m 18f	Dramatic
play	6m 3f	DPS
short play	6m 3f 4 m&f	ICM
musical	11m 3f	MT1
musical	6m 6f, flexible chorus	Dramatic
musical	19m 11f	SF
comedy	3m 7f	SF

TITLE	AUTHOR
Playboy of the Western World, The	J. M. Synge
Playroom, The	Mary Drayton
Plays of America fr. American Folklore	L. E. McCullough
Pledge, The	Victoria Norman
Pollyanna	Catherine Chisholm Cushing
Pool's Paradise	Phillip King
Portrait the Wind the Chair, The	Y. York
Pot Boiler, The	Alice Gerstenberg
Prank	Richard Kalinoski
Precious Sons	George Furth
Premature Corpse, The	Mike Johnson
Prodigy	Mary Hall Surface
Pullman Car Hiawatha	Thorton Wilder
Pygmalion	Bernard Shaw
Quilters	Molly Newman/ Barbara Damashek
Rabbitt	David Foxton
Rainmaker, The	N. Richard Nash
Raisin in the Sun, A	Lorraine Hansberry
Ravenscroft	Don Nigro
Real Inspector Hound, The	Tom Stoppard
Real Queen of Hearts Ain't Even Pretty, The	Brad Bailey
Rebel Without a Cause	adapt. from James Fuller
Regarding Electra	Maurice Valency
Reindeer Soup	Joseph Pintauro
Remember Me Always	Michael Oakes & Jennifer Wells
Remember My Name	Joanna Halpert Kraus
Rememberer, The	Steven Dietz
Rimers of Eldritch	Lanford Wilson
Rise and Rise of Daniel Rocket, The	Peter Parnell

STYLE	CAST	LEASING
drama	7m 5f	SF
melodrama	7m 4f	SF
collection of short plays	variable	S&K
one-act tragedy	2f	SF
comedy	5m 6f	SF
farce	4m 3f	SF
drama	1m 2f	Dramatic
short play	4m 3f	public domain
drama	7m 5f	SF
comic drama	3m 2f	SF
crime thriller	3m 3f	SF
drama	6m 2f	Anchorage Press
one-act comedy	15m 18f	SF
comedy	6m 3f	SF
musical	7f	DPS
one-act drama	15m 1f	SF
comedy	6m 1f	SF
comedy/drama	7m 3f	SF/ RH
mystery	1m 5f	SF
farce	6m 3f	SF
comedy	4f	SF
drama	13m 10f	Dramatic
drama	7m 8f	DPS
drama	4m 5f	A. Agent
one-act comedy drama	4m 5f	SF
drama	5m 5f	SF
biographical	5m 4f 8 chorus	ICM
drama	7m 10f	DPS
play	5m 5f	DPS

STYLE	CAST	LEASING
comedy	9m 4f	public domain
comedy	6m 8f	SF
comedy	3m 4f	SF
tragedy	17m 4f	public domain
comedy/drama	4m 5f	DPS
musical	11m 9f	SF
drama	22m 3f	SF
comedy	1m 1f	SF
drama	3m 4f	SF
comedy	8m 3f	public domain
drama	2m	DPS
drama	7m 6f	DPS
drama	3m 5f	Baker's
musical	11m 10f	SF
one-act comedy drama	5m 3f	SF
musical	5m 6f	SF
drama	8m	Dramatic
one-act	17m 5f	S&K
drama	8w	Dramatic
drama	2m 4f	DPS
one-act comedy	7m 4f	Dramatic
one-act drama	1m 2f	SF
Victorian melodrama	6-9m 1f	DPS
thriller	5m 2f	DPS
drama	1m, 2f	SF
comdy	1m 7f	DPS
musical	6m 6f variable chrorus	Dramatic

STYLE	CAST	LEASING
one-act comedy	2m 1f	Baker's
drama	12m 8f	SF
fantasy	5m 5f	SF
comedy	6m 2f	SF
mystery	4m 1f	SF
comedy/drama	variable	Dramatic
comic drama	2f	SF
comedy/drama (scenes and monos)	10-20	Dramatic
one-act	1m 1f	ICM
musical	9m 15f	RHML
drama	8-17m 3-4f	DPS
black comedy	4m 4f	SF
mystery/drama	4m 4f	DPS
Christmas drama	5, 13-52 extras	Dramatic
one-act	8m 10f	S&K
drama	4m 5f	DPS
drama	3m 3f	SF
monologues	3m 2f	SF
drama	31m 6f	SF
comedy	11m 21f	DPS
drama	9m	SF
musical	6m 6f	SF
play	20m 5f	SF
plays	6f	DPS
narrative theater	min. 3m 3f, flexible	DPS
short play	1m 1f	DPS
drama	16m 11f	SF

TITLE	AUTHOR
Suicide in B-Flat	Sam Shepard
Take a Giant Step	Louis Peterson
Tale of Two Cities, A	adapt. Fitzgibbons
Talking Bones	Shay Youngblood
Talking Pictures	Horton Foote
Talley & Son	Lanford Wilson
Tartuffe	Molière
Tartuffe	adapt. by Noyce Burleson
Teach Me How to Cry	Patricia Joudry
Teahouse of the August Moon, The	John Patrick
Tears of My Sister	Horton Foote
Teechers	John Godber
Tell Me Another Story, Sing Me a Song	Jean Lenox Toddie
Tell Me that You Love Me, Junie Moon	D. D. Brooke from Kellogg
Ten Little Indians	Agatha Christie
Tenth Man, The	Paddy Chayefsky
Tevya and His Daughters	Arnold Perl
There's a Boy in the Girls' Bathroom	Louis Sachar
Thin Air: Tales from a Revolution	Lynne Alvarez
Third Daughter, The	Mario Fratti
This Is a Test	Stephen Gregg
Three Musketeers, The	Peter Raby
Three Ways Home	Casey Kurtti
Throne of Osiris, The	L.E. McCullough
Thurber Carnival	James Thurber
Tide of Voices, A	Suzanne Granfield
Tiger at the Gates	Christopher Fry, trans. from Jean Giraudoux
Time Out for Ginger	Ronald Alexander
'Tis a Pity She's a Whore	Ford
To Be Young, Gifted, and Black	Lorraine Hansberry

STYLE	CAST	LEASING
mysterious overture	3m 2f	SF
drama	7m 7f	SF
drama	16m 10f	SF
drama	2m 3f	Dramatic
drama	6m 5f	DPS
drama	6m 6f	DPS
comedy	8m 4f	SF
one-act farce	5m 5f	Dramatic
play	3m 7f	DPS
comedy	18m 8f, 3children 1goat	DPS
one-act drama	3m 4f	DPS
comedy	2m 1f	SF
one-act	2f	SF
drama	6m 6f	Dramatic
mystery	8m 3f	SF
comedy	12m 1f	SF
play	6m 6f	DPS
comedy/drama	5m 8f	SSA
drama	10m,5f	JKA
drama	3m 4f	SF
one-act comedy	13-15, flexible	Dramatic
drama	20m 5f	DPS
drama	1m 2f	SF
one-act	7m 7f	S&K
musical	4m 4f	SF
drama	4m 1f	SF
tragedy	15m 7f	SF
comedy	5m 5f	DPS
tragedy	mix	public domain
biography	2m 4f	SF

STYLE	CAST	LEASING
one-act drama	4f	Dramatic
play	2m 5f	Broadway
drama	11m 6f	Dramatic
drama	5m 3f	DPS
comedy	13m 8f	SF
nine one-acts	variable	SF
short play	21m 4f	ICM
one-act	min / max 30 m&f	S&K
drama/comedy	3m, 4f	SF
musical	4m 4f	SF
monologues	2m 3f	SF
comdy	11m 3f	public domain
drama	12m (f)	Dramatic
one-act drama	3m 4f	SF
romance	11m 3f	public domain
romance	13m 7f	public domain
comedy	8m 2f	WM
drama	15m 6f	SF
comic drama	5m 4f	SF
comedy	12m 18f	Dramatic
musical	4m 18f	SF
drama	8m 10f	Dramatic
drama	6m 4f	DPS
one-act min	9 / max 25 m&f	S&K
biblical	18m 6f	SF

TITLE	AUTHOR
Villeggiatura: A Trilogy	Goldoni, tr. R. Cornthwaite
Virgin of Orleans, The	Friedrich von Schiller, trans. by Johanna Setzer
Voice of My Own, A	Elinor Jones
Voices from the High School	Peter Dee
Voices from Washington High	Craig Sodaro
Wait until Dark	Frederick Knott
Waterworks	E. J. Safirstein
Way Deep	Katherine Burger
West Side Story	Laurents and Sondheim
Whadda 'Bout My Legal Rights	Marshall & Andrew Lauren Goldman Duxbury
What Did We Do Wrong?	Henry Denker
What I Did Last Summer	A. R. Gurney
When People Could Fly	L.E. McCullough
When They Speak of Rita	Daisy Foote
Whisperings in the Grass	Suzanne Granfield
White House, The	A. E. Hotchner
Who is Chasing Whom!	Lynne Alvarez
Who Will Carry the Word	Delbo
Whodunnit	Shaffer, Anthony
Who's Crazy Now!	Gerald Bell
Whose Life Is It Anyway?	Brian Clark
Why Do We Laugh?	Stephen Gregg
Wild Oats	James McLure
Windshook	Mary Gallagher
Wiz, The	William F. Brown, Charlie Smalls
Women and Wallace	Jonathan Marc Sherman
Woodman and the Goblins, The	Don Nigro
Woolgatherer, The	William Mastrosimone

STYLE	CAST	LEASING
comedy	8m 3f	S&K
romantic tragedy	20m 6f	SF
drama	min. 5f	DPS
comedy/drama	flexible	SF
drama	7m 8f	Dramatic
mystery	6m 2f	DPS
one-act comic drama	1m 3f	SF
one-act drama	3m 2f	SF
musical	27m, 9f, & chorus	RH
musical	3m 3f	SF
comedy	5m 3f	SF
play	2m 4f	DPS
one-act	6m 7f	S&K
drama	3m 2f	Paradigm
drama	5m 1f, guitarist	SF
history	7m 3f	SF
one-act	2m or 2f	JKA
play	23f	Agent
mystery/comedy	7m 3f	SF
farce	3m 9f	SF
drama	9m 5f	Dramatic
drama	4m 4f	Dramatic
comedy	23m 6f	DPS
drama	4m 3f	H&CA
musical	11 various	SF
drama	1m 4f	DPS
one-act dark comedy	1m 3f	SF
drama/love story	1m 1f	SF

STYLE	CAST	LEASING
comedy	9m 7f	DPS
musical	4m 2f	TW
one-act	7m 7f	S&K
drama	21f	DPS
thriller	4m 4f	SF

Play
Synopses

100 LUNCHES
Jack Sharkey & Leo W. Sears   comedy
3m 3f   SF

100 Lunches: Chuck Reynolds is a successful mystery playwright whose critic-nemesis shows up at his door with the chutzpah to ask for his help with her own play. Chuck accepts on the condition that Ms. Charity Starr take him to lunch at the finest New York restaurants for the tutorials. Soon love blossoms, zany waiters abound, and Ms. Starr finds out what it's like to be on the receiving end of the critics' corner. Hilarity and romance combine to make this an ideal family show.

1940S RADIO HOUR, THE
Walton Jones   musical
10m 5f   SF

1940s Radio Hour: The setting is a live broadcast of a musical variety show in December of 1942. A cast of unforgettable characters takes you back in time; with songs like "The Chattanooga Choo-Choo" and "The Boogie-Woogie Bugle Boy," this lively and theatrical show provides an hour of pure entertainment.

A

ABE LINCOLN FOR THE DEFENSE
L.E. McCullough   one-act
18m 4f   S&K

A true-life biographical drama about one of the country's most famous and revered Presidents. The play centers upon a time in Lincoln's career when he was one of the most successful and respected lawyers in the state of Illinois. The case involves the death of a town bully and a young man who hit him with his slingshot. The play is clever and inspiring, and it features a surprise appearance by Mark Twain as a court reporter.

ABIE'S IRISH ROSE

Anne Nichols   comedy

6m 2f   SF

When Abraham Levy brings home Rosemary Murphy, an Irish-Catholic girl he met in France when she was an entertainer and he was in the A.E.F., he introduces her to his father as Rosie Murphyski. The hilarious war between the two lovers' fathers begins when Mr. Levy discovers that his new daughter-in-law is not the nice little Jewish girl he thought. Three weddings and a set of twins (Rebecca and Patrick Joseph) later, the family feud pauses long enough for the play to end and the audience to catch its breath.

ADVENTURES OF HUCKLEBERRY FINN

Randal Myler   comedy

10m 4f   Dramatic

Based on Mark Twain's novel, *Adventures of Huckleberry Finn* has taken the story of Huck Finn and Jim, an escaped slave, and brought them to life on stage. Follow Huck and Jim as they travel down the Mississippi, trying to escape their past and discover themselves. This play leaves out none of the wit and humor for which Twain is famous—a play that truly captures the spirit of the novel.

ADVENTURES OF TOM SAWYER

Timothy Mason   short play

30 mixed cast   ICM

Narrated by a character playing the author, this adaptation of Mark Twain's classic novel brings the flavor of the Mississippi River to life. Tom Sawyer and his friend Huck Finn are constantly in trouble. The boys are good hearted, and often do as much good as they do bad. They are the sole witnesses to a grisly murder and Tom's testimony puts him in great danger with Injun Joe, the murderer. The adventure heightens as Tom and his friends get lost in the mazelike caves, find treasure, and confront Injun Joe when they are most vulnerable.

THE AFRICAN COMPANY PRESENTS RICHARD III

Carlyle Brown   drama

5m 2f   DPS

The African Company, the first all-Black theater troop, battles prejudice and problems from within as they perform *Richard the Third* in competition with the ruthless Stephen Price. Shakespeare becomes the forum for cultural debate in this history-based play that tackles social as well as theatrical concerns.

AFRICAN TALES: KALULU AND HIS MONEY FARM AND RUMPELSTILTSKIN

Timothy Mason   short play

11 m&f   ICM

These two plays are arranged in the form of the African mask and dance with lots of song and movement. The first story takes place in a wonderful kingdom of animals where everyone is happy. The king gives each animal a seed to plant for crops except the bragging rabbit who promises to grow an impossible crop of gold coins. Trapped in his lies, Kalulu the rabbit finally realizes that lies bring only trouble, worry, and a sore hide.

The second tale is the well-known story of Rumpelstiltskin. The king of the land wants to marry a girl who isn't ordinary. The miller claims that his daughter can spin straw to gold. With the help of a little man named Rumpelstiltskin, the girl manages to live up to her father's promise—for a price. She must promise more and more to the little man for his help. Luckily, the girl finds a way to meet her debts, and her husband learns that she is extraordinary, even if she can't spin straw to gold on her own.

AFTERNOON OF THE ELVES

Y. York   drama

1m 5f   Dramatic

York's adaptation of Janet Taylor Lisle's Newbery Award–winning book will touch your heart as two young girls from very different backgrounds befriend each other and discover a secret world in the process. Jan and Alison are stars of the fourth grade; they have recently allowed Hillary to join their ranks. Sara Kate is an upperclassman who has been held back for a second try in the fifth grade. Mr.

and Mrs. Lenox are Hillary's parents. Mrs. Connolly is Sara Kate's mother; she is a person unable to cope.

AH WILDERNESS!
Eugene O'Neill comedy

9m 6f SF

This comic favorite involves an ordinary family in small-town America. The rebellious Richard—a high school senior with a taste for Shaw, Wilde, and Swinburne and a fervent dislike of capital—is in love with the neighbor's daughter. When her father forces them to part, the passionate Richard runs astray and into the company of a strange lady. Finally the faithful damsel sets Richard right and his parents remember what it was like to be young again.

ALADDIN AND THE WONDERFUL LAMP
Timothy Mason short play

30 mixed cast ICM

All the magic of the Arabian Nights are in this play about a young boy named Aladdin, an evil sorcerer, and a magic lamp. The sorcerer pretends to be Aladdin's Uncle in order to get the boy to fetch him the lamp. The sorcerer's plan goes awry, and Aladdin is left with the lamp. He discovers its powers one day as he rubs the dirt off of it, and his life is never the same. The Jinn of the lamp helps Aladdin to win the hand of the princess, but in the end it is his own wit and courage that save the kingdom and defeat the evil sorcerer once and for all.

ALBUM
David Rimmer comedy

2m 2f DPS

Album's eight scenes follow the lives of two teenaged couples as they deal with coming of age in the 1960s. Unfailingly funny and poignant, this portrait of four young people's high school years includes a range of settings and incorporates the music of the times, including Dylan, the Beatles, and the Beach Boys.

ALL'S WELL THAT ENDS WELL
William Shakespeare   comedy
10m 4f   public domain
The troubling story of a girl who is married to a man who does not love her.
Through a series of tricks, she gets him to give her both his ring and a child, the
two conditions under which he said he would truly be her husband. Features one
of the strongest Shakespearean female roles.

ALMOST AN EAGLE
Michael Kimberly   comedy
5m   SF
A witty comedy about an old Boy Scout troop leader trying to hold his scouts
together—even though they would rather be drinking beer than hearing about
upholding the Boy Scout Code. After a disastrous Memorial Day ceremony, the
four boys rally around their fired leader in a poignant and uplifting ending.

THE AMERICAN DAME
Philip C. Lewis   comedy (play out)
                                                                  2m 3f
DPS
The American Dame is the story of American Womenhood. Beginning with the
beginning, the play chronicles the ever-changing and elusive concept of the
American woman. From Eve to the Puritans and the Suffragettes, the play is inter-
laced with excerpts from journals, letters, and biographies that create a rich and
witty look at the American Dame: where she came from, how far she has come,
and where she is headed.

THE AMERICAN PRIMITIVE OR JOHN AND ABIGAIL
William Gibson   history
4m 4f   DPS
The American Primitive follows the lives of John and Abigail Adams as they participate in the founding of a nation. This compelling work offers a unique way in
which to experience history through the eyes of two of America's most intriguing

figures. John and Abigail Adam's own words come to life interspersed with rhymed commentary.

AMULETS AGAINST THE DRAGON FORCES
Paul Zindel   drama
9m 3f   DPS

Amulets Against the Dragon Forces is the touching story of Chris Boyd, a troubled youth and his relationships with Harold, a young hustler; his mother, a divorced nurse who cares for terminally ill patients; and Floyd, the alcoholic son of Mrs. Boyd's patient. The play focuses on Chris's friendship with Harold and its breakdown over the course of the play. The end of the play, however, lends hope that through self-awareness and courage, Chris will escape the lovelessness and loneliness of his childhood—the dragons of his past.

ANALIESE
Lynne Alvarez   drama
8m 8f flexible   JKA

Two teens living in 19th century Denmark are separated when the boy, Christian, mysteriously departs with Nina, an exotic older woman. The girl, Analiese, fearing Christian may be in danger, begins to search for him in a small boat, her only traveling companion being a small insightful toucan. Alvarez reveals a world that is boldly theatrical and classically intelligent.

ANASTASIA
Guy Bolton   drama
8m 5f   SF

The story of Anastasia, the young girl who claims to be the only surviving child of the last Russian Czar, has fascinated millions of people. In this superb drama, a former prince, now a Berlin taxi driver, manipulates a young girl claiming to be the orphaned Anastasia. In the breathless climax of the play, Anastasia must face her grandmother in order to claim the fortune waiting for the children of Czar Nicholas.

THE ANASTASIA FILE
Royce Ryton   drama
2m 2f   SF

The mystery of Mrs. Manahan, the woman claiming to be Anastasia, comes to life in this thrilling and clever play that attempts to solve the case of Czar Nicholas's remaining child. Only four actors play an entire cast of compelling characters, holding the audience spellbound as the story comes to a stunning conclusion.

AND NEVER BEEN KISSED
Aurand Harris   comedy
5m 7f   SF

In this clever and fast-paced play, Flory Patterson, who is almost sixteen and never been kissed, devotes all her time in search of the elusive Opposite Gender. A cast of hilarious characters includes Flory's best friend Millie, her mother, her little sister, and, of course, the parade of boys. Set in 1928, this delightful comedy is both humorous and nostalgic, perfect for students and audiences alike.

...AND STUFF...
Peter Dee   comedy
flexible   SF

Using monologues and short scenes, this challenging collection offers young actors a chance to reflect on the difficulties of growing up in our time. Easy to produce, ...and stuff... lends a voice to today's teens in a variety of deliberately challenging roles created specifically for high school students.

...AND THE RAIN CAME TO MAYFIELD
Jason Milligan   drama
6m 3f   SF

Set in 1962 during the Civil Rights Movement, this powerful and touching play takes place in a gas station/restaurant in Mississippi. Carl Murphy, a teenager who aspires to leave home and go to college, must fight his alcoholic father, Jack, for control of his own destiny as his mother struggles to keep the family together. The catalyst of the play is Nathan, a young black man whom Carl befriends in spite of his father. At the end of the play, Jack must come to terms with his own self, and Carl bravely leaves home to follow his dream.

AND THEY DANCE REAL SLOW IN JACKSON

Jim Leonard, Jr.   **drama**

3m 4f   **DPS**

And They Dance Real Slow in Jackson is the provocative story of Elizabeth Ann Willow, a young polio victim living in Jackson, Illinois. The play focuses on the narrow-mindedness of the small town inhabitants who isolate Elizabeth Ann because of her wheelchair and leg braces. The play chronicles the young girl's descent into madness and the callous townspeople's fear of the "other" that she represents. Through a series of interlocking scenes, this touching play attempts to reveal the prejudice and cruelty too often found in all of us.

ANDROMACHE

Euripides   **tragedy**

4m 5f   **public domain**

Euripides' immortal tragedy, *Andromache,* relates the fateful web of frenzied emotions that lead to murder and betrayal. Andromache, the widow of the slain Trojan hero, Hector, marries her captor Pyrrus in order to save her son's life. Hermione, Pyrrus' betrothed avenges her jealousy by persuading the besotted Orestes to kill him and commits suicide in repentance. The tempestuous emotions that churn around the title character make this play one of the true classics of Greek drama.

ANIMAL FARM

adapted by Nelson Bond   **reading**

5m 2f   **SF**

Nelson Bond has charmingly adapted George Orwell's cutting satire of Communism, *The Russian Experiment,* and all its lies. From the thrill of freedom to the collapse of idealism, this dramatic reading of Orwell's classic allegory introduces a cast of animals that will speak to the audience in a unforgettable combination of drama, comedy, and truth.

ANNA K

Eugenie Leontovich   drama
6m 5f   SF

Eugenie Leontovich has brought Leo Tolstoy's brilliant novel to life in this extraordinary adaptation of *Anna Karenina*. An unexpected and fascinating variation of one of the most important novels ever written.

ANNE OF GREEN GABLES

L. M. Montgomery   musical
12m 17f   SF

Donald Harron's adaptation of L.M. Montgomery's well-loved novel, *Anne of Green Gables*. With music by Norman Campbell, audiences will find themselves mesmerized by the story of an orphan girl who finds happiness through the extraordinary power of her own character. The perfect show, combining music, laughter, and pathos into one unforgettable evening.

ANOTHER COUNTRY

Julian Mitchell   drama
10, flexible   SF

The scene is an English public school in the 1930s where Britain's finest are being prepared to be tomorrow's leaders. The main characters include two outsiders: a young boy struggling with his sexuality and another boy who believes in Marxism. This subtle and political play provides challenging roles in a provocative setting.

ANTIC SPRING

Robert Nail   one-act comedy
3m 3f   SF

This one-act play is staged simply with six chairs designed to create the impression of a open car. Inside are six teenagers going on a picnic. The six characters—Robert, the sensitive boy. Blossom, the idiotic but lively girl; the two lovers; and the younger brother—all provide a fast-paced and flippant show with endless performance possibilities.

ANTIGONE

Sophocles   **tragedy**

3m 3f 10, chorus   **public domain**

Sophocles' classic Greek tragedy about the young girl torn between her duty to the King and her duty to the gods and to her brother. Antigone is the daughter of Oedipus whose sons have both been killed in a bitter civil war. Creon, their uncle, becomes King and decrees that the traitorous son be left unburied. Antigone's individualism and Creon's pride create the inevitable and tragic conclusion to this timeless classic.

ARIA DE CAPO

Edna St. Vincent Millay   **poetic fantasy**

4m 1f   **SF**

Written by Edna St. Vincent Millay, this poetic fantasy involves two shepherds who, with the urging of a masque of tragedy named Cothurnus, interrupt a harlequinade. After they mistakenly kill each other, the harlequinade continues. A rich and fascinating play with unique performance possibilities.

ARSENIC AND OLD LACE

Joseph Kesselring   **comedy**

11m 3f   **DPS**

Arsenic and Old Lace, a comedy favorite for years, is the story of two charming ladies who have the unpleasant habit of storing the remains of their boarders in the cellar of their house. Other characters include the delightfully zany brothers, one of whom thinks that he is Teddy Roosevelt.

AS YOU LIKE IT

William Shakespeare   **comedy**

16m 5f   **public domain**

A comedy that centers around the romantic notion of love at first sight. Devoted lovers Rosalind and Orlando have both fled to the forest in order to escape family members who plot against them. Rosalind, in disguise, tests Orlando and finds him true. He escapes the evil plotting of his brother Oliver, and she the plotting of her uncle who has usurped her father's title of duke. Order is restored in the final scenes when all disguises are cast aside and four happy couples marry as the false duke relinquishes all claims of the title to his brother.

ASCENSION DAY
Timothy Mason   **comedy**
4m 5f   **DPS**
Ascension Day is the haunting story of nine teenagers who spend a week at a summer camp on the edge of a beautiful lake. The play centers on two sisters, Faith and Charity, who are desperately seeking love and approval in the face of their father's frozen nature. Set against the "flying saucer" scare that emerged in the 1940s and the rich traditions of the Native-American population that used to inhabit the lakeside scene, this play concerns itself entirely with the nine children and, although the looming presence of the adults is felt, they are never seen.

ASHES, ASHES, ALL FALL DOWN
Joseph Robinette   **drama**
6m 4f   **Dramatic**
Based on the true story of the tragic deaths of six young people crushed by a crowd awaiting the start of a rock concert, this highly dramatic play deals with the deaths of the six teens as well as the four people trying find a reason for their deaths. The play deftly handles the issues of hero worship, the need to belong, and the breakdown of relationships using humor, hope, and insight.

AUGUST SNOW
Reynolds Price   **play**
2m 3f   **DPS**
August Snow is set in a small, North Carolina town in August of 1937. Here live Neal Avery; his mother the proud and domineering matriarch of the family; his new bride, Taw, a former school teacher; and his boyhood friend, Porter. As the play progresses Taw and Neal have drifted apart as Neal has chosen long nights of drinking while Porter is over spending time with Taw. When she hands him an ultimatum over supper one night, Neal must finally grow up and examine his life as it really is.

B

THE BALD SOPRANO

Eugene Ionesco   comedy

3m 3f   SF

Ionesco's brilliant comic satire attacks the English middle class and the dreariness of their lives. With humor and wit, Ionesco brings to light the inherent flaws in communication that plague the characters—and an entire class of people.

BALLROOM

Jerome Kass   musical

14m 17f   SF

Based on the book by Jerome Kass, this superb musical was developed by award-winning director Michael Bennett. It tells the story of a widowed grandmother who wants to start living again; she attends the Stardust Ballroom, falls in love, and scandalizes everyone but herself and her lover.

BARNUM

Brum, Stew, & Coleman   musical

11m 8f   TW

This highly theatrical circus musical traces the career of P. T. Barnum, the World's Greatest Showman, from his beginnings as a promoter of sideshows to his great museum in New York and to the cofounding of the famous Barnum and Bailey Circus.

THE BARRETTS OF WIMPOLE STREET

Rudolph Besier   romantic comedy

12m 5f   DPS

The Barretts of Wimpole Street is a romantic comedy about Elizabeth Barrett and her family. Set in young Elizabeth's room, the play centers around the father's tyrannous control over the family and Elizabeth's determination to find love and happiness. Although she has never been healthy, Elizabeth, through the help of the young poet Robert Browning, comes to realize that she need not spend her life under the unloving yoke of her father. Despite many obstacles, the two lovers eventually escape Wimpole Street to start a new life.

BEAUTY AND THE BEAST
Timothy Mason   short play
8m 6f   ICM

When a merchant gets lost in the woods and takes a rose for his daughter Rose from a rich estate, he is forced to trade rose for Rose to the estate's angry owner. Rose goes to live with the Beast in his giant castle and lives a life far easier than her former life at home—except that she misses her family desperately. The Beast is really a prince trapped in a spell that can only be broken by Rose's true love. Her love is put to test when first her father, and then the Beast become fatally ill.

BECOMING MEMORIES
Arthur Giron   drama
5m 5f   SF

Based on true stories, this ensemble piece follows the changes in small-town America by tracing three families through five generations. This is a rich play that allows each of the ten characters to play several parts. A simple and powerful story, *Becoming Memories* reveals the values and people that give midwestern America its distinct flavor.

BELOVED FRIEND
Nancy Pahl Gilsenan   drama
13m 9w   Dramatic

Beloved Friend is the story of two young pen pals, Kristin, who has been encouraged by her high school to correspond with a young girl from Rhodesia, and Rachel, the young African who must struggle against poverty and indignity. The two girls' lives are played out on a divided stage that reveals the growing bond between the two girls even as the distance between them may grow. Over the course of the play, Rachel becomes a high official in the new Rhodesian government and comes to America on business, where she realizes that she has not heard from Kristin. Rachel finds her in a coma with multiple sclerosis and only her love can bring Kristin back.

BENEFACTORS
Michael Frayn   drama

2m 2f   SF

This is the story of an architect who starts out believing in the power of environment, trades in this belief for the scheme forced upon him, and watches the new set of ideals fall. Examining the difference between doing good and being a do-gooder, this comic drama speaks to everyone who has tried to change the world only to have it change you.

BEST CHRISTMAS PAGEANT EVER, THE
Barbara Robinson   x-mas comedy

12m 15f   SF

A lively alternative to the old Christmas favorites, *The Best Christmas Pageant Ever* is the story of a husband and wife who try to put on a play and who are forced to cast the meanest kids in town. This hilarious and fun-filled play has great roles for young actors and provides rich holiday entertainment for everyone.

BEYOND THE FRINGE
Bennett, Cook, Miller & Moore   comedy

4m   SF

A hilarious revue written by four brilliant comedians. A variety of performance opportunities including a preacher, a Shakespearean spoof, and a skit with three nuclear scientists determined to talk about the issue to death.

BIG BLACK BOX, THE
Cleve Haubold   short play

1m, one box   SF

The Big Black Box has only a bare stage and two characters, Arnold and the black box that also serves as the only prop. Arnold is thin and soft-spoken; he isn't very bright although he doesn't acknowledge that fact. The box begins talking to him and slowly Arnold is drawn toward it. He keeps giving the box money and other belongings, at first to see what's inside and then to buy his freedom. Finally, during the moment of his triumph when he has propped the lid open with his umbrella, the box swallows him.

BIG MARY
Mark Medoff   **drama**
10m 10f. flexible   **DPS**
Big Mary is the story of a circus elephant and her attempt to prevent her trainer from marrying and leaving her. Set in the small town of Eddington, Tennessee, this play touches upon racial prejudice, mob mentality, and the fear ignorance can create. When the unhappy Mary kills her trainer's unsavory assistant, the townspeople decide, in spite of an orphaned black girl's wise protests, to hang her. Originally written for high school performers, this play contains many powerful roles for young actors.

BILLY LIAR
Willis Hall & Keith Waterhouse   **comedy**
3m 5f   **SF**
Billy Fisher is a teenager who, finding his life and his job—as an undertaker's assistant—boring, retreats to a world of lies and daydreams until reality and fantasy become hopelessly and irrevocably intermingled. Even when young Billy has the chance to redeem himself through an opportunity provided by one of the three girls to whom he is engaged, he rejects the chance and clings to his dreams.

A BIRD OF PREY
Jim Grimsley   **drama**
4m 4f, chorus   **Gersh**
When Monty's family moves from Louisiana to a large city in Southern California, he and his siblings encounter a dangerous landscape where cruelty thrives among their peers, offering little comfort from their abusive home life. This gripping drama embraces the good and evil young people face alone in their lives.

BLESSINGS
Mary Hall Surface   drama
3m 4f   S&K

Blessings looks at the forging of an unlikely bond between two very different four-teen-year-old girls — one a driven over-achiever, one a gifted artist with severe learning disabilities.

BLUE DENIM
James Leo Herlihy & William Noble   drama
3m 3f   SF

An insightful play about the generation gap, *Blue Denim* examines true-to-life characters: young people who are not delinquents and parents who are not uncaring, but generations who cannot understand each other. The story focuses on a fifteen-year-old boy who gets his girlfriend pregnant and through this crisis he and his parents discover that they never really knew each other.

THE BODY AND THE WHEEL
William Gibson   play from Gospels
min. 24   DPS

The Body and the Wheel is the story of Jesus of Nazareth. Taken from the gospels, the play chronicles Jesus' life up to the time of the Crucifixion and the Resurrection. A fast-paced and truly dramatic play that brings the Gospels and the teachings of Jesus to life.

BONE-CHILLER!
Monk Ferris   comedy/mystery/thriller
5m 8f (flexible)   SF

This comedy-mystery-thriller starts out like any other mystery play but soon twists and turns until the audience finds itself just as eager and unable to solve the mystery as the hapless characters. The play involves the reading of a will, an impossible riddle, sudden blackouts, and chilling murders. An unforgettably entertaining evening of theater.

BORN GUILTY

Ari Roth — drama

4m 3f — SF

The dramatic adaptation of Peter Sichrovsky's compelling novel. The play follows Sichrovsky's journalistic exploration to interview the sons and daughters of Nazi officials and his own obsession with finding the people who killed his grandmother. What he finds is a woman to help him overcome the hatred he has uncovered and the obsession he can't leave behind.

THE BOYS NEXT DOOR

Tom Griffin — comedy

7m 2f — DPS

The Boys Next Door takes place in a New England city. Under the watchful eye of the earnest but worn Jack, a young social worker, four mentally handicapped men live together in a communal residence. There is Norman who revels in the bunch of keys that hang from his belt; Lucien P. Smith who believes that he can actually understand the weighty books he carries about; Barry, a brilliant schizophrenic who thinks that he is a golf pro; and their leader, Arnold, a hyperactive talker who suffers from a persecution complex. Poignant and funny, this play brings understanding to what it means to be handicapped.

BREAKING THE PRAIRIE WOLF CODE

Lavonne Mueller — play

2m 4f — DPS

Set in 1866 on a wagon train headed west, *Breaking the Prairie Wolf Code* is the story of a young widow and her frail daughter looking to start a new life. Helen, a pampered Easterner, must face the harsh realities of the trip: lost food and clothes, illness, and demanding physical trials while still taking care of her sick daughter. Eventually misfortune forces the other travellers to leave them behind and the play ends with the two women stoically facing death.

BREAKING THE SILENCE
Stephen Poliakoff   drama

3m 4f   SF

A strikingly original play about the challenges faced by Poliakoff's upper-middle-class family in post-Revolution Russia. Forced to live in a railway carriage as the father secretly tries to record sound onto film, this clever and fascinating play follows the family until Lenin's death and their flight from Russia.

THE BRIDE OF BRACHENLOCH!
Rick Abbot   Gothic thriller

3m 8f   SF

A hilarious complication of the Gothic set-up, this play offers a range of zany characters. With plot twists, suspicion, intrigue, and romance, this play is too good to spoil. Goofy Gothic fun for performers and audiences alike.

BRIGHTON BEACH MEMOIRS
Neil Simon   comedy/drama

3m 4f   SF

Neil Simon's semi-autobiographical account of his teenaged years. It is the story of Eugene, a young Jewish boy living in a lower-middle-class family and struggling for understanding and dignity in a world of poverty and hardship.

BROKEN RAINBOWS
Mary Hall Surface   drama

2m 2f   S&K

Broken Rainbows offers producers a no-punches-pulled look at the complicated issue of hate-violence.

BROTHER GOOSE
William Davidson   comedy

3m 9f   Dramatic

Brother Goose is a delightful comedy about Jeff Adams, an architect who must take care of his orphaned brothers and sisters. Into his life walks Peggy Winkel who sells hosiery but who is mistaken for the new maid by a frazzled Jeff. Romance and humor abound in this easily produced play.

BULLSHOT CRUMMOND
Ron House farce
3m 2f SF
This parody of a low-budget film is a farcical detective story from the 1930s. Bullshot Crummond is the "hero" of this play; he attempts to save the kidnapped Professor Fenton from the evil Otto van Bruno and his mistress. In spite of his hopeless incompetence, both Crummond and this play triumph in the end with hilarity and wit.

BYE BYE BIRDIE
Stewart, Strouse, & Adams musical
22m 26f TW
A musical spoof of "Elvismania," *Bye Bye Birdie* is about the hysteria surrounding a teen singing idol's last appearance before his induction into the army. When rock star Conrad Birdie gets drafted, his manager arranges a nationwide competition in which one lucky girl wins a farewell kiss on the *Ed Sullivan Show.*

BY HEX
Renier, Blankman, & Gehman musical
9m 5f DPS
In *By Hex,* Jonas, a young Pennsylvania Amish man, rebels against the strict codes of his religion as does Nancy, the Bishop's eldest daughter. Both the young people are shunned when Jonas buys a tractor in an attempt to go modern and then forces the Bishop to shun his daughter who was caught kissing a non-Amish man. Nancy's younger sister, who cannot marry her sweetheart Eli until Nancy is married, tries to bring the two rebels together using a Hex as Jonas is the only Amish man who could even speak with Nancy. Eventually Nancy and Jonas realize their love for each other and two marriages end the play.

C

CAESAR AND CLEOPATRA
Bernard Shaw   comedy
20m 5f   SF

In Shaw's version of the age-old legend, Cleopatra is not yet the grand, seductive queen but rather a frightened girl of sixteen. Caesar, the Roman general, attempts to reconcile the two factions that threaten to rip Egypt apart while trying to stay alive in the sea of political turmoil. Both the title characters have much to learn from each other in the world of politics. When a truce is made, the land is made one, and Caesar is ready to sail for home, Cleopatra exacts a promise from him to send in his stead another young Roman—Mark Antony.

THE CAGE
Mario Fratie   drama
5m 3f   SF

The Cage is the dramatic story of a young Chekhov devotee who has misunderstood the great playwright's philosophy. The young man, Cristiano, insists upon living in a cage and refuses to communicate with anyone. His more pragmatic and humorous family tries to convince him that he needs to experience and enjoy life, but it is Chiara, the voluptuous wife of his brother, who manages to get through to him. When he realizes that he loves her, he kills his own brother and asks Chiara to open the cage. The young woman, while grateful for her release from an unhappy marriage, goes onto another lover, and Cristiano is fated to live the rest of his life in the cage.

THE CAINE MUTINY COURT-MARTIAL
Herman Wouk   drama
19m   SF

The Caine Mutiny Court-Martial has been adapted by the author of the Pulitzer Prize–winning novel, to tell an exciting tale of adventure on the high seas during World War II. The play dramatizes the court-martialing of a young lieutenant who relieves his captain of his duties aboard their ship during a typhoon. Though tradition and the rules are against him, the young sailor and his witnesses manage to convince the jurors that the Captain's behavior had put the entire ship in danger. This is a fast-paced and highly dramatic version of the classic story.

CAMILLE

Alexandre Dumas trans. Henriette Metcalf   drama

11m 6f   SF

A translation of the classic French drama by Alexandre Dumas, *Camille* tells the story of the doomed love between a Parisian courtesan and the son of a Marquis.

CAN'T BUY ME LOVE

Jason Milligan   one-act comedy

3f   SF

A comedy about three high school friends: Ellen,the bossy know-it-all; quiet Amy; and Sandy the peacemaker. Bored in their dull Mississippi town, they realize one night that Paul McCartney is worth 600 million dollars and decide to call him and ask him for a million dollars. Of course, Ellen suggests that Amy, who has secretly been in love with the Beatles since she was six, be the one to call him since she needs to be cured of her fear of boys. Surprisingly, Amy does get through to the rock star and all three girls learn the oft-repeated phrase that money can't buy happiness—or love.

CAROUSEL

Rodgers & Hammerstein   musical

12m 7f   RHML

Billy Bigelow is a smooth-talking carnival barker who falls in love with a mill-worker on the coast of Maine at the turn of the century. Shortly before the death of his daughter, Billy is killed while committing a robbery. Now in heaven, Billy returns years later to earth for one day to attend his daughter's high school graduation and to teach her one very important lesson.

CATCH 22

Joseph Heller   comedy

9-36m 2-8f   SF

Joseph Heller has written a wonderful adaptation of his classic spoof on war and capitalism. Told from the point of view of Captain Yossarian, a pilot convinced that every flight will be his last. Other characters include: a mess officer who runs a cartel in scarce commodities, a Roman prostitute, an Army nurse with whom Yossarian is briefly in love, undercover agents who investigate each other, and the ex-PFC who actually runs the war by deciding where the mail goes.

CATHOLIC SCHOOL GIRLS

Casey Kurtti   comedy

4f   SF

An excellent play that reveals what life in the sixties was really like. The four female actors play the schoolgirls from first through eighth grade as well as various teachers. Each character also performs several monologues interspersed with the scenes. This satirical play delves into sixties culture—from the Beatles to the Addams Family to JFK—while expressing with timeless accuracy the joys and insecurities of youth.

CAT'S PAW

William Mastosimone   drama

2m 2f   SF

Mastrosimone's gripping play about terrorism focuses on the cat-and-mouse game between a young woman reporter and the brilliant, articulate Victor who is obsessed with the pollution of the world's water supply. Victor leads a group responsible for a bombing attack on the White House in which twenty-seven innocent people are killed. The dialogue between the reporter and Victor provides superb dramatic material for young actors.

CEREMONIES IN DARK OLD MEN

Lonne Elder   **drama, Black Groups**

5m 2f   **SF**

Ceremonies in Dark Old Men is a portrait of life in the ghetto and the story of a family who longs for a better life but goes about finding it in a tragic way. The family owns a barber shop but has no customers, the sons are shiftless, and only the daughter keeps the family together. Other characters include a crone, a girl who has "been around," and the Prime Minister of the Harlem Decolonization Association. A dramatic play that has been compared to *A Raisin in the Sun*.

CHAT BOTTÉ (PUSS IN BOOTS)

Pamela Gerke   **one-act**

min 7 / max 25 m&f   **S&K**

In *Chat Botté* it's obvious that the cat is indeed the master of his human owner. In this story from France, youngest Enfant obeys his magical cat and is rewarded with wealth, prestige, and true love.

CHEAPER BY THE DOZEN

Christopher Sergel adapted from Gilbreth & Carey   **comedy**

9m 7f   **Dramatic**

This comedy is based on the book by Frank Gilbreth and Ernestine Gilbreth Carey. The main character of this play is Anne, an attractive high school girl whose father is one of the pioneers of industrial efficiency and the head of a very large household. When Dad tries to implement his industrial management in his family life, comedic disaster ensues. Anne and Dad seem unable to understand each other and Dad's secret heart condition doesn't help. Finally, however, he realizes how much his little girl has grown up—a sure audience pleaser.

THE CHERRY ORCHARD

Anton Chekhov   **drama**

9m 5f   **DPS**

The setting of this play is the family estate of Madame Ranevskaya, an estate famous for its cherry orchard. The action begins with Madame Ranevskaya's return from Paris where she has spent the last of her fortune on a young lover. Instead of facing the impending loss of the estate for delinquent taxes, she and her friends and family continue to live as if nothing were wrong. Only the eventual buyer of the land, the nouveau-riche merchant, Lopahkin, realizes the gravity of the situation. At the bittersweet end of the play, the cherry trees are felled and Madame Ranevskaya leaves for Paris once again.

CHILDREN OF A LESSER GOD

Mark Medoff   **drama**

3m 4f   **DPS**

The play centers around James, a young speech therapist, and Sarah, a hearing-impaired young woman who has rejected the hearing world entirely. James tries to draw Sarah back into the world and the two slowly fall in love and marry, but as the play progresses Sarah's increasingly militant approach to the rights of the deaf causes a rift between them. Only love and compassion can hold the two together, and the audience is left with hope for a fuller understanding between the two worlds.

THE CHILDREN'S HOUR

Lillian Hellman   **drama**

2m 12f   **DPS**

A serious play about two women who run a school for girls. When a malicious young student starts a rumor about them, the scandal precipitates tragedy for the innocent women. Even when it is discovered that the rumor was pure invention, irreparable damage has already been done.

CHOICES

Walden Theatre Young Playwrights   **comedy/drama**

10-20   **Dramatic**

Choices is a collection of monologues, scenes, and ten-minute one-acts for young actors that explores friendship, love, parents, alcoholism, and the pains of growing up. This collection, authored by a group of Walden Theatre Playwrights, ranges from the serious and dramatic to the lighthearted and comic. Can be presented together for an evening of entertainment or as short showcases for young talent.

THE CHOPIN PLAYOFFS

Israel Horovitz   comedy

5m 3f   DPS

A play about the lives of Jewish families living in Sault Ste. Marie, Ontario, after the Second World War. Stanley Rosen and Irving Yanover are boyhood friends, but manhood finds them pitted against each other. First, the two are piano prodigies and will compete with each other for a prestigious prize. Second, both men are in love with the same (non-Jewish) girl, Fern Phipps. Friendship wins the day when they both conspire to play poorly; and as Fern has declared she will choose the winner of the contest for her beau, obstacles are cleared and a lesson in friendship, family values, and love is learned.

CLASS ACTION

Brad Slaight   collected

3m 4f   Baker's

A collection of scenes that can stand by themselves, *Class Action* is connected by the common thread of dealing with situations that occur outside of the high school classroom—situations that are often the most meaningful or most difficult for young people. Scenes include one in which a young man gets himself two weeks of detention to be with a girl he likes; a monologue where a young woman talks about her unexpected pregnancy; and another scene in which a pretty popular girl and and an unpopular guy stand up to their friends and admit that they care for each other.

CLASS DISMISSED

Craig J. Nevius   comic drama

13m 12f   SF

Far more than a typical "high school" play, this comic drama was written by a nineteen-year-old high school graduate. The story centers around a frustrated high school teacher who, in an attempt to fight the apathy he sees in his students, takes his toughest students hostage in a classroom. The students singled out are a conceited jock, the obnoxious class clown, the prom queen, and the sensitive intellectual.

CLEVELAND

Mac Welman   short play
3m 7f   ICM

Joan is a teenage girl whose father has died and who now lives alone with her eccentric mother. Joan is upset because she won't get the prom date she wanted because she and her mother are no longer fashionable. This fantastical play uses dream sequences and the possibility that Joan and her mother are creatures from another planet to suggest the awkward and complicated process of growing up.

THE CLUB

Eve Merriam   musical
flexible   SF

The setting of this "musical diversion" is a stuffy, all-male club where the members dress in top hats and tails to sing fourteen songs from the 1894–1905 period. Both the songs and the conversations between the members indicates that these chauvinistic men believe that male superiority will live on forever—with women as mere side dishes and where suffragettes need to keep their places. In the surprise ending, however, we find that these smug men are really women!

COCKEYED KITE

Joseph Caldwell   drama
8m 5f   DPS

Jeff, a young teenager, learns that he doesn't have long to live and so decides to spend the little time left to him finding out who he is. He embarks on a mission to find his real father's identity. The ensuing scenes are touching and funny as Jeff must deal with his family, friends, and sexual awakening. By the end of the play, Jeff has truly found himself and is left free of his search, free to fly.

THE COLORED MUSEUM

Wolfe   drama

2m, 4f   GA

The Colored Museum consists of eleven satirical sketches that turn popular African-American stereotypes and cultural icons on their heads. Some of the skits include a business executive and his alter ego, a young street kid; a Vietnam veteran who has died only to gain insight into the treatment of Black vets; two empty-headed *Ebony* models; and a pair of wags. A diverse assortment of characters provides humorous material with a serious message.

COLORED PEOPLE'S TIME

Leslie Lee   Black history

6m 3f   SF

This extraordinary historical play traces African-American history from the Civil War to the Montgomery Bus Boycott nearly one hundred years later. This concise, economical play uses thirteen vignettes set at the moment of a major social change. Each tiny vignette uses a different fictional character to trace the history and spirit of Black America.

COME SLOWLY, EDEN

Norman Rosten   drama

5m 2f   DPS

A portrait of the secretive New England poetess, Emily Dickinson, *Come Slowly, Eden* tries to uncover the mystery behind one of America's most talented women writers. The play begins after her death at the moment in which Emily's sister discovers her poems hidden in a bureau drawer. The play follows her life through the poems, letters, and memories of her family. From her childhood to unrequited love, and withdrawal, this is a vivid portrait of a woman born before her time.

COMEDY OF ERRORS

William Shakespeare   comedy

11m 5f   public domain

There is no need for deliberate trickery in this comedy of mistaken identities. Two sets of twins, separated from birth, find themselves in the same place. No one realizes that there are two sets of identical men, who also happen to have the same names, wandering the city. The result is mass confusion in this lighthearted comedy.

COMPETITION PIECE

John Wells   **one-act comedy**

10-21, various   **SF**

Well-suited for a high school competition play. A clever comedy about three high school drama groups trying to put on three separate plays. The first group has an abundance of time and chooses a romance to perform; a second group, made up of typical meathead-type characters, chooses a stereotypical teen-problem play; and the last group, the artsy set, decides to do a one-act King Lear as a Japanese Noh drama.

THE CONTRAST

Royall Tyler   **comedy**

5m 4f   **SF**

The very first American comedy ever written, *The Contrast* deals with the question of whether or not Americans should try to develop a culture of their own or whether they should follow the customs of the British. The contrast to which the title refers is between those Americans who donned heavy powdered wigs and English affectations and the more rough-and-ready colonists who wanted to strike out on their own. This refreshing musical version preserves the original charm and wit of Tyler's play.

COURTSHIP

Horton Foote   **drama**

3m 5f   **DPS**

The setting of this play is a warm spring night in Harrison, Texas, in 1914. At a party in the home of the well-to-do Vaughns, their daughter Elizabeth and her sister gossip about the other party-goers. Although the God-fearing and rather restrictive morals of the Vaughns seem oppressive to the romantically inclined Elizabeth, through the conversations that emerge in the play, we find that the older generation was vulnerable to the same temptations that now threaten the peaceful life of the Vaughns. Elizabeth, over her family's objections, is determined to marry the rakish Horace Robedaux. In the end, however, she does not quite have the courage to escape the gentle but firm hold that her parents and their way of life has upon her.

COWARDLY CUSTARD

Noel Coward   **revue**
6m 6f   **SF**

A musical revue of the words, sketches, and music of Noel Coward. *Cowardly Custard* includes his classic music as well as unpublished materials: bits of plays and dialogues, and excerpts from his biography and poems. The result of this collection is a masterful glimpse at the achievements of Noel Coward—pure entertainment that offers a variety of performing opportunities.

THE CRADLE SONG

G. Martinez-Sierra, trans. Underhill   **romantic**
4m 10f   **SF**

The Cradle Song is the story of an infant brought to a convent and how her presence affects the lives of the nuns who rear her. As the young girl grows up and the nuns lavish all the human love and affection on her that is absent from their own lives, the extraordinary changes in the nuns' lives become apparent. When the infant has become a young woman, however, she falls in love and leaves her home. This romantic play is told with grace and pathos within a simple framework.

THE CRUCIBLE

Arthur Miller   **drama**
10m 10f   **DPS**

A powerful historical drama and a parable of our modern society, *The Crucible* tells the story of the Puritan purge of witchcraft in old Salem. The story centers around a young farmer whose wife has been maliciously—and wrongly—accused of witchcraft by their young servant girl. The climax of the play is the trial scene where the farmer tries to make the girl admit her lies and instead is himself imprisoned and condemned along with his equally innocent wife. A gripping chronicle of the power of bigotry and deceit.

CRY HAVOC

Allan Kenward   drama
13f   SF

Cry Havoc is the dramatic story of a group of medics trapped on Bataan. The characters are trapped in a dugout where they are subjected to gunfire, and the play follows their reactions to the war. Characters include: a strong-minded doctor, her reserved and poised assistant, and the volunteer nurses.

LA CULABRA (THE SNAKE)

Pamela Gerke   one-act
min 5 / max 25 m&f   S&K

A trickster story from the Aztec culture, this tale is about the aftermath of a windstorm where a snake has been wrapped around a tree and the countryside put topsy-turvy. The question the play sets out to answer is whether or not something bad will happen to you if you do a good deed.

THE CURIOUS SAVAGE

John Patrick   comedy
5m 6f   DPS

Honesty and kindness battle greed and dishonesty in this fanciful comedy about a woman who inherits ten million dollars from her late husband. Mrs. Savage, newly rich and widowed, wishes to establish a fund to help others fulfill their dreams, but her greedy stepchildren are determined to get their hands on the money and have her institutionalized in an attempt to "bring her to her senses." In the sanitarium, Mrs. Savage meets people who have been unable to adjust to society but who befriend her for who she is and not how much money she has. When her doctor tells her she should be out in the real world, only with the help of her friends can she defeat the stepchildren's plotting and fulfill her dreams—as well as theirs.

D

DA-HOOS-WHEE-WHEE (THE SEAL-HUNTING BROTHERS)

Pamela Gerke   one-act

min 10 / max 35 m&f   S&K

This story tells the epic journey of two intrepid brothers who are bewitched by
the evil grandfather of their sister's husband. The brothers go on a spirit journey
into the unknown and come home empowered, singing their spirit songs of
strength and energy.

DADDY LONG LEGS

Jean Webster   comedy

6m 7f   SF

The charming story of Judy, a pretty New England orphan who charms a visiting
trustee. The anonymous benefactor becomes known by Judy as Daddy Long Legs.
The orphans appear in only the first act and their ages are flexible. Most of the
play focuses on the romance that develops at the fashionable college Judy is able
to attend with the help of Daddy Long Legs.

DADDY'S HOME

Ivan Menchall   one-act drama

1m 1f   SF

In this award-winning play, a teenaged boy and his mother prepare to pack up
their belongings and move from their house. The premise of the play is that
Daddy is not home, and he has left his wife and only son to deal with their own
feelings of rejection, confusion, and loss.

DAGS

Debra Oswald   comedy

4m 6f   Dramatic

The protagonist of this play is Gillian, a sixteen-year-old "dag,"—misfit, nerd,
outcast. Gillian sees herself as ugly and socially crippled. The play follows her as
she deals with her bright, popular, and optimistic sister; her gossipy friends; an

addiction to chocolate; and a hopeless crush on the school's heart throb. In the surprise ending, however, Gillian triumphs over it all with an unforgettable moment of self-awareness.

DAMES AT SEA

George Haimsohn, Robin Miller, Jim Wise   **musical comedy**
4m 3f   **SF**

An award-winning musical comedy based on the Hollywood musicals of the 1930s with a very flexible cast. Set in The Big Apple, a hometown girl meets a hometown boy: She as an aspiring star and he as a sailor and aspiring songwriter. In true Hollywood style, love is threatened by the wiles of the show's female star but wins the day when the sailor saves the show with his new song, and the sweet hometown girl sings it from the deck of a passing battleship.

THE DANCE AND THE RAILROAD

David Henry Hwang   **one-act drama**
2m   **DPS**

As their fellow Chinese workers go on strike to protest the railroad's abuses, Lone practices the art of Chinese opera and his pupil, Ma, struggles to win at first Lone's help and finally his approval. The abuse that Lone piles on Ma is part of his plan to rid him of his innocence and test his character, but Ma perseveres and convinces Lone that he has the strength to become an actor, just as the Chinese workers win their strike.

THE DANCERS

Horton Foote   **one-act drama**
3m 7f   **DPS**

A short play set in Harrison, Texas, in the early 1950s. The play focuses on Horace, a young man who has come to visit his sister for two weeks. The married, meddling sister has set up a date with Horace and Emily, the most popular girl in town. Emily refuses to go to the dance because she is going steady with another boy. Love blooms, however, between Horace and Mary Catharine, a pretty but poor girl who shares and understands Horace's lack of confidence.

DANCING FEATHERS

Kleitsch and Stephens   drama

                                                                  Annick

Christel Kleitsch and Paul Stephens's *Dancing Feathers* is the touching story of Tafia, a young Ojibway girl. Tafia lives on a reserve in Thunder Bay, Ontario, Canada, and struggles to balance the demands of the modern world with the rich but threatened culture of her people.

DANCING SOLO

Mary Hall Surface   drama

2m 3f   Dramatic

Dancing Solo follows sixteen-year-old Kara's struggle to choose the right steps in her difficult dance of life with her alcoholic mother and her wayward boyfriend. With the help of her dance instructor, Kara is able to break through her naiveté and deal with the painful truths.

DANCING WITH STRANGERS

Sandra Fenichel Asher   trilogy of short plays

3m 6f   Dramatic

A trilogy of short plays that are connected by the common theme that life is an intricate and confusing dance. In the first play, *Blind Date,* the main character, Dawn Covington must face her feelings of betrayal and confusion after her parents' divorce as well as deal with her emotional dependency on her mother. In *Perfect,* Tara Owens looks to a stranger to give her a cure for her loneliness—she becomes pregnant by a classmate whom she barely knows. The last play, a hilarious and energetic play called *Workout!* we see boy meet girl, lose girl, and get her back all in the course of one aerobic dance class.

DARK OF THE MOON

Howard Richardson & William Berney   drama

28 roles   SF

A play based on the ballad of "Barbara Allen" that uses a large cast and includes a rich variety of folk songs. The play tells the story of an elfin witchboy who falls in love with the beautiful, human Barbara Allen. A deal is made that as long as she remains true to him, the elf can take on a human form and become her husband. When the marriage is consummated, Barbara Allen gives birth to a witch-child whom the midwives burn. In the tragic ending, Barbara Allen dies, after betraying her husband who then returns to his true form.

DAUGHTER OF A TRAVELING LADY
Peter Dee   one-act comedy-drama
1m 2f   SF

A compassionate and insightful study of the strength and loneliness of a young teenager. The young woman has been conditioned by her haphazard upbringing to be independent and self-sufficient. The play begins with her arrival at her suburban home where she awaits the arrival of her wandering and frequently absent parents. Other characters include another teenage girl and a young telephone repairman, both of whom try, unsuccessfully, to manipulate her. With comedy and sympathy this play examines the essential character of one lonely teenager.

DAVID AND LISA
Theodore Isaac Reach adapt. James Rubin   drama
11m 11f   SF

A simple, easy-to-produce play that tells the story of two mentally ill adolescents. David, the son of wealthy but domineering parents, is haunted by his fear of being touched. Lisa is a young girl who has never known parental love and who has developed a split personality: one side of her speaks and demands to be spoken to in childish rhymes. The play takes place in Berkely Hospital where the two young people have come under the sympathetic guidance of psychiatrist Alan Swinford. Other characters include: Carlos, a street urchin; the over-romantic Kate; stout Sandra; and other students as well. Follow David and Lisa through exhilarating ups and depressing lows of a world about which most of us know very little.

¿DE DÓNDE?
Mary Gallagher   drama
8m 5f   DPS

This compelling drama is perfect for young actors. It concerns itself with the plight of Mexican immigrants and their desperate need to escape the poverty of their homeland by avoiding the officials of the Immigration and Naturalization Service (INS). The title of the play refers to a shortened version of the Spanish phrase, "Where are you from?"—a question that is the first phrase heard by Hispanics whom the INS suspects of being illegal immigrants. The play takes place in the Rio Grande Valley of Texas, a home for many Mexican refugees.

DEAR RUTH

Norman Krasna   comedy
5m 5f   DPS

A popular romantic comedy about a young girl who writes to a soldier overseas. The letters, however, are written in the name of her older sister—who is already engaged. When the young man returns home, he, of course, comes to see and to woo the elder sister. After a series of complications and hilarious plot twists, the sister becomes convinced that her first engagement was a mistake and finally decides to marry the soldier instead.

DEATH IN SCARSDALE

Victor Levin   one-act comedy
3m 2f   Dramatic

David R. Irkman is dead. After his divorce form the only woman he would ever love, he ran his Plymouth into a Scarsdale telephone pole. His ex-wife Robin, loved him—but was not in love with him because he smothered her with his love: She tells him that he could drive even a plant out of the house if he decided to love it. Unfortunately, Robin was the only thing in this world that was real to him. Sympathetic and hilarious with great roles for young actors.

DEATH TAKES A HOLIDAY

Alberto Cassella   drama
7m 6f   SF

A novel play that develops the poetic conception of Death taking a three-day holiday during which he falls in love with a beautiful girl. Through his relationship with her, he comes to realize why mortals fear him. This simple love story is appealing and avoids any of the conventions that could have been dragged in for mere effect. Death becomes very human and the play presents an optimistic philosophy on the problems of love and death.

DEEP BLUE FUNK AND OTHER STORIES

Daniel B. Frank and Arnold April   one-act drama

1m 4f   Dramatic

With a flexible cast and a simple set design, this play is perfect for schools and communities who want to discuss the problems of teenaged pregnancy with honesty and sympathy. The play presents real-life histories of young people who must deal with becoming parents as they themselves are still growing up. The stories transcend the boundaries of the African-American community in which it is set and portray the innocence, love, fear, and anger of the characters. The play comes with background information, discussion questions, and classroom activities.

DESIGN FOR MURDER

George Baston   Thriller

4m 6f   SF

A fast-moving and surprising thriller. The main character of the play is Celia Granger who lives in her old family mansion on the Hudson River with her son David. Trying to preserve the traditions of her family, Celia is abruptly torn from the past when a young maid is killed. Suspicion falls on everyone in the cast and in the climax, Celia is alone in the house with the murderer ready to strike again. Comedy is supplied in the form of two women friends and romance in the shape of the rugged detective who had admired Celia in the past.

DIAMONDS

collaborative   musical revue

7m 3f   SF

This musical revue was created by a Hall of Fame ensemble from contemporary American musical theater. Contributors include: Betty Comden, Adolph Green, John Kander, Fred Ebb, Howard Ashman, Craig Carnelia, Alan Menken, Jim Wann, and more. The revue is composed of comic songs and ballads interspersed with sketches that create a perfect montage of all that is baseball. Baseball buffs and non-fans alike will enjoy this good-natured celebration of America's favorite pastime.

THE DIARY OF ANNE FRANK

Frances Goodrich and Albert Hackett   drama
5m 5f   DPS

This acclaimed play has won the Pulitzer, the Tony, the Critics' Circle, and many other awards. A dramatization of the story of Anne Frank, a young Jewish girl growing up in the days of Hitler and the Holocaust. The play is based on the book, edited by Anne Frank's father, Otto Frank.

THE DINING ROOM

A. R. Gurney   play
3m 3f   DPS

Set in the dining room of a wealthy family, this play chronicles the lifestyle of a dying breed—the upper-middle-class WASP. In a series of alternately funny and touching vignettes, the actors play a series of characters from a giggling teenager to a senile grandmother and from a stern grandfather to a little boy. A great opportunity for actors to portray a variety of characters, this play becomes a sketch of an entire pattern of American life.

DINO

Rose, Reginald   drama
8m 10f   Dramatic

Dino, the main character of this play, is a complicated young man who presents a difficult problem for his family, friends, girlfriend, and for himself. At the young age of seventeen, Dino has just been released from reform school after four years. His parole officer is tough, sympathetic, and competent, and he realizes that something must be done to prevent Dino from becoming a hardened criminal. Made for young actors and deeply relevant for young audiences.

THE DISAPPEARANCE OF THE JEWS

David Mamet   **one-act drama**

2m   **SF**

An unusual one-act play that focuses on a discussion/debate between two men, both of Jewish heritage. The discussion touches upon the various events in their past and the contemporary meaning and relevance of these events and of their own Jewishness.

LA DISPUTE

Marivaux, trans. Timberlake Wertenbaker   **comedy**

mix   **Dramatic**

A one-act translation of Marivaux's classic comedy. A Prince has brought his love, Hermione, to a strange garden enclosed by high walls. The garden has been built to settle a dispute that began years ago in this very same kingdom and has now been renewed by the Prince and Hermione. The dispute centers on the origin of infidelity: Did it begin with man or with woman? Inside the garden are two men and two women and, in an attempt to re-create the Garden of Eden, they have been raised in total innocence. When the Prince and Hermoine arrive, they are to meet for the first time and settle La Dispute.

THE DIVINERS

James Leonard   **drama**

6m 5f   **SF**

The setting is a small Indiana town in the 1930s. *The Diviners* is about a mentally disturbed boy and his relationship with a disenchanted preacher. The boy, who is deathly afraid of the water, almost drowned as a child and lost his mother in the same accident. The preacher, who comes from a long line of preachers, is determined to break away from the profession he does best; he becomes a mechanic for the boy's father. The townspeople want a preacher and the preacher wants the boy to overcome his fear of water. In the climactic ending, the preacher takes the young man to the river, and the townspeople, mistaking the washing for a baptism, rush into the river as well. In the ensuing confusion the young man is drowned.

DO YOU SEE WHAT I'M SAYING?

Megan Terry   drama

7f   SF

Set in Chicago in 1991, this play is a multicultural play based on actual interviews with homeless women. The action of the play takes place one morning as we meet each of the seven women: The Copper Queen, a down-on-her-luck prostitute; B.A. and Crissie, two enterprising garbage pickers; Mychelle and Himilcé, two drug addicts, one of whom wants to be clean; Valrave, an intense but burned-out sex kitten; and Sunny, who spontaneously shouts out sermons

DOES A TIGER WEAR A NECKTIE?

Don Peterson   drama/comedy

14m, 3f   DPS

The setting is a drug rehabilitation center—really more like a prison—for young junkies of both sexes and all races. The main characters are an English teacher in the center; Tiger, a malicious, cocky student; and the establishment's psychiatrist who forces Tiger to tell him his "story." Other characters include a black prostitute, a black junkie who might just make it clean, a veteran official of the center, and a perverted, cynical rebel. This play offers many slices of life with brutal honesty and insight.

A DOLL'S HOUSE

Henrik Ibsen   drama

3m 4f   SF

The classic feminist play about a woman who loved her husband enough to commit forgery for him and about a husband who treated his wife like a plaything, to be wound up and set out on demand. Finally, the young wife realizes that she does not need this arrogant man she has married and leaves him to his surprise and dismay.

A DOLL'S HOUSE

Henrik Ibsen adapted by Albert Pia   one-act drama

3m 3f   Dramatic

A one-act version of Ibsen's classic, feminist play about a woman who loved her husband enough to commit forgery for him and about a husband who treated his wife like a plaything, to be wound up and set out on demand. Finally, the young wife realizes that she does not need this arrogant man she has married and leaves him to his surprise and dismay.

DON JUAN

Molière trans. by Albert Bermel   satirical drama

18-20m 3-4f   SF

A translation of Molière's satiric drama, *Don Juan* contains two of the most memorable characters in Molière's plays: Don Juan, the rebel who pursues every beautiful woman he meets and delights in defying the conventions of his society; and his servant Saganarelle, a voice of respectability and conformity throughout the play. The satire attacks everything from religious hypocrisy to the legal and medical professions. Entertaining, gripping, and filled with acute observation about not just Molière's society—but about ours as well.

DON'T COUNT ON FOREVER

Nancy Pahl Gilsenan   drama

6m 8f   Dramatic

The story of Lisa, a talented high school senior who thought that she could always count on a good future, a good family, and good friends. She suddenly has to confront her parents impending divorce, a zany newspaper staff of which she is the chief-editor, and graduation. When commencement arrives, her father Frank has left, but although everything Lisa came to count on is breaking up, she refuses to be defeated and delivers a remarkable address to the senior class.

DON'T DRINK THE WATER
Woody Allen   **comedy**
12m 4f   **SF**

A zany comedy that takes place in an American embassy behind the Iron Curtain. An American tourist who is a caterer by trade and his wife and daughter rush to the embassy two steps ahead of the police who have accused them of spying and picture taking. The embassy proves to be poor refuge as the ambassador is out of town and his son—already expelled from Africa and a dozen countries—is in charge. In spite of these obstacles and in the midst of their plot to escape, the caterer's daughter and the ambassador's son have time to fall in love.

DOROTHY MEETS ALICE
Joseph Robinette   **musical**
11, flexible   **Dramatic**

What happens when the Yellow Brick Road leads into the Rabbit Hole? This wonderfully hilarious comedy is about the meeting between two of literature's most famous young ladies—Alice and Dorothy. The two characters have met and their stories become intertwined when a contemporary boy puts off a book report until the last minute. All the familiar characters are present: the Cowardly Lion, the White Rabbit, the Tin Man, the Mad Hatter, the Scarecrow, the Dormouse, and the Queen and the Witch. A fanciful musical all audiences will enjoy.

DOWN FROM THE SKY
Geraldine Ann Snyder & Paul Lenzi   **musical**
3m 2f   **Dramatic**

A musical with a message written for contemporary young audiences, *Down From the Sky* focuses on the pressures and consequences of teenage drug abuse. Ronny, a high school student, has begun to use drugs and is considering quitting school to work for Chick Waldo, a, local drug dealer. Both Ronny's friends and his sister become concerned with his behavior through the course of the play. With humor and music, this play makes the warning about drug abuse easy to follow and to believe.

DRACULA

Christopher Nichols   one-act thriller

5m 1f or 2m 4f   Dramatic

A one-act adaptation of Bram Stoker's classic tale. Fast-paced, nonstop action begins with the entrance of Professor Van Helsing, who has come from London to help his friend and student, Dr. Seward, cure the mysterious illness of Mina Murray. Mina is about to marry Jonathan Harker, but Dracula has other plans. Fortunately the monster is no match for the aging Professor as this Gothic tale ends in the classic style.

DREAMTIME DOWN UNDER

L.E. McCullough   one-act

4m 2f   S&K

Intended for a very young cast. Perhaps the oldest surviving mythology in the world is that of the aboriginal people of Australia. Central to aboriginal mythology is the "Dream Time," an ancient time when the ancestors travelled across Australia shaping the landscape, structuring society, and depositing the spirit of unborn children in animals, trees, and people. It is believed that the energy of an ancient being can be released by rubbing or striking the place where he or she left the world: Anyone born at that site becomes a guardian of that spirit. The play has a narrator who takes us through each adventure.

DUTCHMAN

Baraka (formerly LeRoi Jones)   drama

2m 1f   SF

A thought-provoking and disturbing short play. A lascivious blonde attracts the attention of a decent young Black man on a subway car. Failing to seduce him, she humiliates him until he descends to her level, declaring that all Blacks should rise up against all Whites. Finally, she stabs him and as other Whites on the subway dispose of his body, she primps for her next victim.

THE DYBBUK

S. Ansky   **drama**

24m, 7f   **SF**

This brilliant translation of Ansky's tragic play tells the story of the love between
Channon and Leah. Having been denied Leah's hand in marriage in favor of a
wealthier suitor, Channon turns to the dangerous magic of Kabala in hopes of
winning her love but dies in the mystical attempt. In death, Channon returns as
a dybbuk, or evil spirit, and possesses Leah on her wedding day.

E

EAST OF THE SUN, WEST OF THE MOON

Pamela Gerke   **one-act**

min 7 / max 50 m&f   **S&K**

This Norwegian tale is an intergalactic version of *Beauty and the Beast*. A handsome prince has been turned into a bear by a princess with a long nose. His only hope is to find another princess who will fall in love with him, and who will seek him out among the stars on the Blue Planet.

ECHOES

Vaughn McBride   **evening of monologues**

variable   **Dramatic**

Echoes is a series of monologues written by the author from his experiences working with young playwrights and actors. Though the material may be used as audition competition pieces, they are meant to be performed as an event, as a showcase for young talent. The diversity of the monologues and their number make them very flexible as to the type of event presented.

EDDIE "MUNDO" EDMUNDO

Lynne Alvarez   **drama**

3m 3f   **JKA**

The story of a Hispanic boy's journey back to Mexico to find the past that he has lost and to sort out the future he has after the death of his mother. The play centers on the deep conflicts between his native culture, in New York City's Hispanic population, and his roots in Nautla, Mexico. In Mexico he stays with his aunt Chelo and her fiancé of many years, Nyin, where he meets and falls in love with a local girl, Alicia. A touching story of searching for identity and belonging.

EDUCATING RITA

Willy Russell   **drama**

1m 1f   **SF**

Frank is a disillusioned English tutor in his fifties who has taken to the bottle.

Along comes Rita, a forthright, twenty-six-year-old hairdresser who is hungry for an education. She fascinates Frank with her shrewdness and refusal to accept a second-rate education. Through the course of the play she reinvigorates Frank with her zest for life and makes him believe in himself once again.

THE EFFECT OF GAMMA RAYS

Paul Zindel   drama
5f   DPS

This award-winning play tells the story of Beatrice Hunsdorfer, an acerbic, embittered woman who lives with her two daughters and a decrepit old boarder. Beatrice lives by wreaking petty vengeance on those around her, giving hurt when she should give love, and derision when she tries to praise. Her two daughters both suffer under her cruelty: The oldest daughter, Ruth, is pretty but high-strung and subject to convulsions; the younger daughter, Matilda, is painfully, almost pathologically shy, but a gifted science student. When a high school teacher encourages Matilda to enter a contest and she wins with her gamma ray experiment on marigolds, the tragic climax occurs as Beatrice's acerbic and slatternly nature prevent her from caring for her children. Tillie, however, proves both with her experiment and with her actions that a thing of beauty can arise out of even the most barren soil.

ELECTRA

Euripedes   tragedy
5m 2f   public domain

The classic story of Electra, the young daughter of the victorious warrior Agamemnon. Daughter to adulterous Clytemnestra, Electra spent much of her young life waiting first for her father and then for her brother, Orestes, to return and exact revenge for the crimes committed in the house of Atreus.

ENCOUNTER 500

Mario Fratti & Guiseppi Murolo   musical
8m 4f   SF

Set at New York's Public library on 42nd Street, October 12, 1992, the play is a love story between Chris (an Italian-America) and Isa (a Hispanic). While they meet in the library, a parade commemorating Columbus Day is going by. Suddenly, the characters become Christopher Columbus, King Ferdinand, Queen Isabella, and Count Ferdinand. All of the love, doubt, mutiny, and excitement of the Age of Discovery come to life as Columbus, forbidden to love his Queen, falls in love with a native girl whom he names Isabella. Suddenly the action goes back to New York where Chris and Isa have joined the parade, as happy lovers.

AN ENDANGERED SPECIES
Kathy Sorenson   **drama**
3m 4f   **SF**

A drama that effectively shows the dangers and fears surrounding AIDS. The play centers around a group of high school students who discover that they have been spreading the HIV virus through heterosexual sex. The play charts their emotions, from denial to anger, blame, and fear. Each of the young people must face the misunderstanding, prejudice, and mistreatment that HIV positive and AIDS victims must undergo. They must confront the possibility of their own deaths when one of their friends is hospitalized, and in the final scenes, one young survivor reflects on her own treatment of her friend in need and vows to continue the fight for AIDS research and education.

ENEMY OF THE PEOPLE
Henrik Ibsen   **drama**
10m 3s   **S&K**

Ibsen's stirring drama of the battle between truth and self-interest. The setting is a small Norwegian town that has begun to attract wealth and attention by virtue of its medicinal spring waters. When Dr. Stockman, the local physician in charge of the springs, discovers that they are poisoned, he reports his findings to the town officials. Instead of being thanked for his research, Dr. Stockman and his family find themselves hushed, ignored, and finally abused and ostracized from the small community. In the concluding scene, as the doctor and his family face an angry crowd armed with stones, he tells them, "But remember now, everybody, you are fighting for the truth and that is why you are alone. And that makes you strong."

ENTER LAUGHING

Joseph Stein   comedy

7m 4f   SF

Enter Laughing is the hilarious account of a youth who works as a delivery boy for a sewing machine factory but who dreams of becoming an actor. Although his family wants him to become a druggist, the young dreamer saves enough money to enlist in a semiprofessional company that will put anyone on stage for the right price. Unfortunately our hero is a horrible actor and his attempts on stage provide some of the funniest moments of the play. A romantic element is provided by scenes with the manager's daughter, someone else's date, and the office girl who was meant for him.

EQUUS

Peter Shaffer   morality drama

5m 4f   SF

A powerful drama that focuses on Martin Dysart's confrontation with Alan Strang, a young boy who has blinded six horses. To the boy's parents the act is a horrifying mystery and to the owner it was as simple as his mistake in hiring "a loony." To the psychiatrist it is a mystery that, when unraveled, touches his as well as Alan's inner needs and fears. The play confronts the powerful human need for worship and what "civilized" society does to those needs.

EVERY SEVENTEEN MINUTES THE CROWD GOES CRAZY!

Paul Zindel   drama

8m 6f   DPS

In the remnants of a formerly warm and gracious home, fourteen young people have been living without any adult supervision for nearly two months. The teenagers each have their own hopes and dreams: Ulie, the youngest who misses the family; Dave, an attractive older boy; gorgeous Maureen who uses her beauty to get what she wants; and Dan whose glad the family is gone and wants to take over. This is a thought-provoking play about the power and needs of children.

EVERYMAN/EVERYWOMAN

Virginia Egermeir

4m 5f, 6-10 either

modern allegory

Dramatic

A modern remake of the medieval allegory that can be done by either a male or female lead. The tale begins as Everyman (or Everywoman) is given one hour to put his affairs in order. The hero or heroine realizes that taxes and dinner dates are no longer important, and as he tries to find someone to accompany him on his journey, the only taker is Good Deeds, an unselfish, impulsive, and not very bright young lady (or man). All the allegorical figures are represented: Beauty, Strength, Worldly Goods. Medieval speech has been replaced with the contemporary English of a shopping center.

F

FAITH COUNTY

Mark Landon Smith   **comedy**

3m 6f   **SF**

A parody of small-town life, *Faith Country* takes place somewhere in the middle of nowhere down South. In a place where beehive hairdos are chic and Saturday nights are for tractor pulls, everybody has gathered together for the annual county fair. With stiff competition in the arts and crafts department as well as a wedding and an (untimely) birth and death, this play has characters you'll fall in love with. Originally made for radio.

FAME

David De Silva from Christopher Gore   **drama**

9m 15w   **Dramatic**

Developed around auditions for the School of Performing Arts in New York City, this play follows the pursuit of fame in the performing arts. The play follows the growth and struggles of students and their interaction with the teachers who guide them. This is a compelling drama that finds the hearts of young people and the spirit of the theater. A play that can easily be adapted to the needs of the performers.

FAMILY DEVOTIONS

David Henry Hwang   **drama**

4m 5f   **DPS**

Ama and Pop are two elderly Chinese women who live in Bel Air, California. They live there with their daughters and their daughters' rich husbands. Although the daughters have embraced self-involvement and wasteful living, the grandchildren are trying to escape it. When the sisters' brother returns from China, to which he had returned after fleeing because he believed in the Revolution, they are faced with a man they do not know. He no longer believes in God and tells them that the evangelist whom they revered was a fake. The sisters die from the shock as the young people flee from their family.

FANTASTIKS
Schmidt & Jones   **musical**
7m 1f   **MT1**

Musical *Romeo and Juliet* in reverse. This time the families want the children to unite. The Fathers, using reverse psychology, create a feud and "send" their children away. Of course, the children run to each others arms. Mission accomplished! However, Act Two shows the union starting to erode. The Fathers resolve to return to their lives and the Boy walks out on the Girl. He leaves her only to return disillusioned. The couple has suffered but grown up in the process. They reunite. Songs include "Try to Remember," "Soon It's Gonna Rain," "This Plum is Too Ripe," and "They Were You."

THE FATHER
August Strindberg, trans. John Osborne & Harry G. Carlson   **drama**
5m 3f   **SF**

In the grand style of the Greek tradition, this translation of Strindberg's play captures the stark power of the human tragedy. The main character is an Army Captain who battles his wife over the future of their daughter. The awesome struggle drives him mad and he finally succumbs. A powerful drama with compelling characters.

FENG ZHEN-ZHU (THE WIND PEARL)
Pamela Gerke   **one-act**
min 12 / max 40 m&F   **S&K**

An ancient tale from China that follows the classic formula of the hero/heroine on a journey of self discovery. Ha-xin bravely pursues knowledge and enlightenment. Along the way he suffers hardship, meets magical helpers, encounters danger and evil, and is ultimately saved by love. And like the best folktales, the element of magic is vital to both the plot and delightfulness of the story.

FIDDLER ON THE ROOF
Harnick, Stein, & Brock   **musical**
12m 10f   **MT1**

One of Broadway's longest running musicals, *Fiddler on the Roof's* protagonist is Tvye, an embattled Jewish milkman and parent struggling to uphold tradition amidst personal and social upheaval. Set in an increasingly anti-Semitic Czarist Russia, the plot centers on the rebellious marriage plans of his three eldest daughters. Much to their father's chagrin, one weds for love without the customary services of a matchmaker, one weds a Gentile, and the third marries a radical who is soon arrested and sent to Siberia. With his uncertain world perched precariously like a "Fiddler on the Roof," Tvye invokes the sympathetic ear of his God.

FIONN IN SEARCH OF HIS YOUTH

L.E. McCullough   **one-act**

5m 2f   **S&K**

This is a short play based on Irish mythology and intended for a young cast. Fionn Mac Cumhaill and the Fianna and their band of warrior adventurers and how they came to get their special powers and why they are remembered today.

THE FIRST BREEZE OF SUMMER

Lee   **drama (Black groups)**

8m 6f   **SF**

The story of a middle-class Black family in a small northeastern city. The central themes of the play deal with the younger son Lou, who is ambitious and sensitive. He and his family struggle to deal not only with issues of race but also with his sexuality. His relationship with his father's mother, Gremmer, and her reflections on her own life add another rich thread. Other characters include his father, a moderately successful business man, and his older brother Nate.

FIRST IMPRESSIONS

Abe Burrow's adapt. from Austen   **musical comedy**

14m 12f   **SF**

An adaptation of Jane Austen's masterpiece, *Pride and Prejudice,* this play follows the Bennett's attempts to marry their five daughters. It centers around the romance between Elizabeth Bennett and Darcy, a rich arrival in their small town. The other daughters' romances also flourish, adding a rich background to the main plot. There are colorful ball and garden party scenes where many extras may be used.

THE FIRST
Joe Siegel w/Martin Charnin   musical
48m 12f   SF

The musical tale of Jackie Robinson, the first Black man to play major league baseball. It is also the story of Branch Rickey, the first team owner who had the fortitude to ignore tradition and racism and hire Robinson. Adaptable to different cast sizes, this musical captures an important moment in American history in a compelling manner.

THE FLAMES OF HELL (LES FLAMMES D'ENFER)
L.E. McCullough   one-act
8m 6f   S&K

Set in the bayou country of Louisiana, this play about the Cajun music of the region tells the story of a talented musician, Aldus Fontenot. A creative and enjoyable variation of the classic deal-with-the-devil story, the play combines music, comedy, and dance for a large cast.

FLAMING IDIOTS
Tom Rooney   farce
6m 2f   SF

A delicious comedy about two ambitious ex-postal workers who lack the judgment to make their restaurant venture succeed. Carl and Phil decide that, if their rival restaurant, Zippy's, draws so much attention because a notorious gangster was killed there, then perhaps a murder would help their business as well. A contemporary farce that takes place entirely in a kitchen and needs five doors for slamming. This play won the New American Comedy Festival Award.

THE FLIGHT OF ICARUS
L.E. McCullough   one-act
11m 2f   S&K

Short play adapted from Greek mythology. Intended to be performed by a young cast. This play tells of the Labyrinth and the events that led Icarus and his father to be jailed there. True to the classic version, Icarus flies too close to the sun, his wings melt, and he falls to his death in the ocean. Great classic plot and moral—easily understood by a young cast and young audience.

F. O. B.
David Henry Hwang   comedy
2m 1f   DPS

This play explores a contemporary issue in American society. Two cousins, Dale, born in America, and Grace, a first generation Chinese immigrant, find that they must confront their own beliefs about China, America, and their own identities when Steve, a Chinese exchange student comes into their lives. Dale and Steve provide direct conflict while Grace tries to negotiate between the two; she eventually finds herself drawn to Steve and an uneasy truce is found.

FOOLS
Neil Simon   comedy
7m 7f   SF

The story of Leon Tolchinsky, a schoolteacher who arrives at the Russian hamlet of Kulyenchikov only to find that the village is cursed—everyone there is stupid. Leon stays to try to break the curse because he has fallen in love with the beautiful daughter of the local doctor, a young girl who is so stupid she just learned to sit down. Of course our hero breaks the curse and wins the girl. A bright comedy with a fairy-tale quality and morality mixed in for good measure.

FOREIGNER
Larry Shue   comedy
5m 2f   DPS

Another comedy from a lauded comedic playwright. The action takes place in a Georgia fishing lodge where "Froggy" LeSeuer, stationed at the nearby Army base, has brought his pathologically shy friend, Charlie. In order to help Charlie avoid interacting with the other guests, Froggy tells them that he cannot speak English. As the evil guests reveal their secrets and plots to the listening Charlie, the hilarious action rolls toward the climactic ending where the good guys and the bad guys get their just deserts.

FRANKENSTEIN

Tim Kelly drama

4m 4f SF

An entertaining and thought-provoking retelling of Mary Shelley's classic tale. Victor Frankenstein, a brilliant young doctor, has retreated to his Swiss chateau to escape the pursuit of the horrible monster he has created. No one, not even his family or his fiancée, can free him from this dark secret. When the monster arrives and demands a bride to share his life with him, Victor reluctantly agrees. Soon the terror begins anew with murder and thrills to scare and delight audiences.

FREYA'S GOLDEN NECKLACE

L.E. McCullough one-act

4m 4f S&K

This short play is from Norse mythology. Freya is a goddess who possesses a golden necklace. While she has it, peace prevails; should she loose it, chaos would ensue. One day, Thor, god of thunder and lightning, visits Freya to ask her for a favor. His hammer has been stolen and he needs to disguise himself as Freya to be able to enter the home of Thrym, the offender. Thor convinces Freya to lend him her necklace, but Thor forgets to return the necklace.

FULL MOON

Reynolds Price drama

4m 5f DPS

A beautiful play of young love that weaves passion and the fear of growing up into a touching story of two young adults who find themselves and love. Neither Kip nor Kerney knew their mothers, and both must face the fear of leaving their families to start a life together. Kerney's father and their butler make up the family who she still clings to; and Kip's maid, a mother to him, and her daughter, who is more than a sister to him, present another choice for Kip. In the end the moon shines down upon their new beginning, together.

G

GALILEO
Bertolt Brecht   bio
27m 4f   SF

Set in the Age of Reason when Galileo teaches his young students that the earth revolves around the sun and that the moon reflects only the light of the sun. Soon the Church hears of his heretical teachings and he is brought to the Vatican as his friends desert him and his plea to the Pope is intercepted. Although the brilliant scientist is forced to recant, he continues his writings in the seclusion of his prison cell. One of Brecht's finest plays.

GET BILL SHAKESPEARE OFF THE STAGE
Joseph Robinette   comedy
6m 10f   Dramatic

This is a humorous and sometimes bitter confrontation between high school students and their drama teacher who both learn to better understand each other. The students learn to appreciate the Shakespeare they wanted off the stage and the idealistic teacher learns to listen and to understand the students. Complete with lots of lively backstage action and uniquely developed characters, this play is truly a delight to direct and to watch.

THE GIFT OF THE MAGI
adapt. by Anne Coulter Martens   Christmas drama
2m 5f   Dramatic

The touching adaptation of O. Henry's story of a poor young couple unable to afford to buy each other Christmas presents. Unknowingly, they work at tragic yet humorous cross-purposes to sacrifice a treasure and provide a gift for the other. This play is ultimately about love and about giving, both wisely and foolishly.

GILGAMESH AND THE ROSE OF ETERNAL YOUTH
L.E. McCullough   one-act
7m 3f   S&K

Based on a myth from Sumaria, Gilgamesh—King of Uruk—leaves his kingdom
to search for immortality. This epic tale chronicles this unique hero's story of one
of his most famous adventures, surviving a great flood that destroys the human
race, but for one family.

GIRL TALK
Dori Appel & Carolyn Myers   comedy
2f   SF

A fast-paced comedy about the complexities of female friendship. Composed of
seven scenes that include twelve-year-old girls separated by puberty; bosom bud-
dies in their thirties who face the ticking of the biological clock; a little-known
historical moment in the friendship between Gertrude Stein and Alice B. Toklas;
and the last, a scene with two octogenarian friends who plot their escape from a
convalescent home. Very flexible casting and simple staging allow this play to
showcase strong monologue and scene material and allow the actresses themselves
to shine.

A GIRL'S GUIDE TO CHAOS
Cynthia Heimel   comedy
3f   SF

Written by Cynthia Heimel—a delightfully funny feminist who sees men not as
part of the problem but as part of the solution, this play uses material from her
book, *Sex Tips for Girls*. Cynthia and her two best friends, Cleo and Rita find
themselves dealing with the trying times of heterosexual women, including "The
Great Boyfriend Crunch" and other facts of life. Bare stage and vibrant characters.

THE GIRLHOOD OF SHAKESPEARE'S HEROINES
Don Nigro   monologue collection
5f   SF

A collection of five monologue plays that may be performed separately or together.

They represent a compelling and humorous exploration into what it means to be a minor character in someone else's world. Two plays deal with Hamlet's Ophelia; one concerns an aging actress and her obsession with the Lady from the cursed Scottish play; another deals with the nature of obsessive love through the eyes of a minor character in a more obscure Shakespearian work; and the last focuses on Miranda, Prospero's daughter. A great opportunity for young talent that is both funny and touching for contemporary audiences.

GIVE 'EM HELL HARRY

Carl Eugene Bolte, Jr.   documentary drama
14m 6f   SF

An exciting docudrama of the Truman years in the White House. The play deals with this unlikely but talented statesman, the history of his time, and the decisions he was forced to make. Characters include the women in his life who influenced him, his friends, and the other historical greats who composed the personal and political playing field on which he found himself. This play is easily staged and well paced.

GO ASK ALICE

Frank Shiras   drama
8m 15f   Dramatic

This powerful drama of a young girl who inadvertently gets drawn into drug use and abuse is based upon the actual diary of an anonymous girl. The play allows the actors to involve themselves in problems that confront America's youth every day. The lesson of this play is so powerful because it is learned through experience, learned by a teenage peer's real experience and pain. As Alice tries to face her addiction and to find herself, the actors and audience will have a chance to examine their own lives and the decisions that they face. A bare set allows for easy staging. A one-act version is also available.

GOD'S FAVORITE

Neil Simon   comedy
5m 3f   SF

Neil Simon's adaptation of the Book of Job. It takes place in the Long Island mansion of a wealthy tycoon who has a prodigal son and a set of twins. A messenger from God appears and soon everything is a test of faith—his business, his family, and his home. In spite of the many maladies inflicted upon him, Job insists that he has been chosen to show how much a man can love God; he perseveres until God admits defeat. Stunning, real-life humor will make this play a hit for all audiences.

GODSPELL

Schwartz   **musical**

5m 5f   **TMax**

Godspell is a colorful and lively musical based upon the Gospel according to Saint Matthew. The memorable list of songs includes: "Prepare Ye the Way of the Lord," "Day by Day," "All for the Best, We Beseech Thee," and the stirring "Finale."

GOLD DUST

Jon Jory   **musical comedy**

5m 3f   **SF**

Gold Dust is an extremely loose musical variation of Molière's *The Miser* from the Actors Theatre of Louisville. Set in a saloon in a Western mining camp, the action centers around Jebediah Harp who has found gold and wealth but who insists upon hoarding it. A combination of lively music and lyrics, perfect for high school groups and budgets.

THE GOOD DOCTOR

Neil Simon   **comedy**

2m 3f   **SF**

A collection of sketches that include one in which a father taking his son to a house where the son can finally solve the mystery of sex; one of a man offering to drown himself for three rubles; and another where a seducer finds that his victim has been in control from the start. Droll humor mixed with affectionate portraits of Chekhov's tales.

GOOD MORNING, MISS VICKERS
Stephen Levi   comedy
3m 7f or 4m 6f   SF
Five teenagers find themselves trapped in a time bubble. A play that combines ghosts, mystery, and a teacher from every student's worst nightmare into nonstop action and fun as the group of teenagers try to free themselves from the bubble and the ghost school in which they are trapped. This play has received rave reviews from high schools around the country.

THE GOVERNMENT INSPECTOR
Gogol, adapt. by Peter Raby   comedy
20m 8f   DPS
An adaptation of Gogol's comedy, the play's action centers around the corrupt bureaucrats of a Russian hamlet. Horrified to learn that a Government Inspector, in disguise, is about to visit their town, the squabbling officials suspect that a young penniless clerk is the Inspector and begin to shower him with gifts, including a young wife. When they discover the truth, the real Inspector has requested their presence in the name of the Czar.

GREASE
Jim Jacobs & Warren Casey   musical
9m 8f   SF
This well-known and well-loved classic '50s musical has delighted scores of audiences and performing groups. With colorful songs and nostalgic scenes, this musical guarantees fun for all. Danny Zuko, head of his rough-and-tumble gang, and the wholesome Sandra Dee work out their budding young love amidst songs and dancing. The sheer energy of this play makes its production fun and easy.

GREAT EXPECTATIONS
Alice Chadwicke   drama
7m 8f   SF
Adapted from Charles Dickens's beloved novel, this play is the story of Pip. Pip as a young man is apprenticed to a blacksmith and finds himself sent to a wealthy

old maid, Miss Havisham, as a playmate for her young ward—the cold and charming Estella. Longing to be a gentlemen to win Estella's love, his adventures lead to a surprise ending. With all of the wit and insight of Dickens's novel, this play is a true delight.

GREAT SCOT!

Mark Conradt & Gregory Dawson   musical comedy
8m 8f   DPS

A lively musical comedy based on the exploits of the young Robert Burns. It focuses on the romances of the dashing poet. The play follows him from his native village and his love with Jean Armour to Edinburgh and the social world he plunges into. Finally, denouncing the life of debauchery, he returns to his first love who has born him twins. An elegant celebration of youth and spirit.

GREATER TUNA

Jaston Williams, Joe Sears, Ed Howards   comedy
2m   SF

A hilarious portrait of small-town life set in Tuna, the third smallest town in Texas. The catch to this comedy is that all of the characters, from Aunt Pearl to Reverend Spikes, are played by the same two actors. Pulled off with quick costume changes, all twenty characters come to life in a wild production. The play can easily be adapted to use more actors.

GREENFIELD BLOOMS

Michael Oakes & Jennifer Wells   one-act comedy/drama
3m 4f   SF

A motley group of urban youths, led by Danny, attempt to bring some beauty into the world. Clearing an abandoned lot within the dilapidated high-rises of the Greenfield Projects, the intrepid teenagers grow and nurture an urban garden. Soon the president of a clothing conglomerate decides to build on their lot and the action really begins. This play goes right to the heart of life in the city; it is both touching and street smart

GRETA NILSON'S MAGIC MARE

L.E. McCullough   one-act

7m 4f   S&K

Variations of the story about an uncatchable white mustang that might be a phantom or a ghost-horse can be found in the folklore of many Native American tribes. This play is an intriguing interpretation of a Blackfoot tribal legend. It is a gentle and inspiring tale that examines the theme that suggests that primal forces of nature can only be understood and harnessed by those who are pure of heart.

H

HAGAR'S CHILDREN

Ernest A. Joselovitz · **drama**

6m 3f · **DPS**

Bridehaven Farm is a home for emotionally troubled teenagers, run by two caring and compassionate counselors, Oliver, a young Black man, and Esther, a Jewish woman. The action takes place around Christmas Eve as the two counselors realize that the children have become increasingly withdrawn and bitter toward society and toward their parents in particular. This disillusionment climaxes with the brutal slaying of a pet lamb. The subsequent investigation, led by the children, allows them to take a giant step toward understanding and rehabilitation. An astounding play, filled with compassion and poignancy.

HALF A SIXPENCE

Beverly Cross · **musical**

12m 11f flexible chorus · **Dramatic**

At the turn of the century at a seaside resort in England, Kip and his fellow apprentices work away; his main concern is Ann, his young love to whom he gives half a sixpence as a token of his love. When Kip inherits a fortune, however, their promise is forgotten as he is swept up by new, rich friends. Just as he is about to marry a society girl, he again finds Ann who offers to return the sixpence. Love prevails in the end of this delightful musical with a captivating score.

THE HAPPIEST DAYS OF YOUR LIFE

John Dighton · **farce**

7m 6f · **SF**

A lighthearted farce, set just after the Second World War, examines what happens when a boys' and a girls' school are set to join. The arrival of the parents complicates the action as neither the headmaster nor the mistress wants them to know that the school is now coed. Only the threat of a third school joining bonds the two warring groups together. A whimsical look at the breaking down of gender differences.

THE HAPPY JOURNEY TO CAMDEN & TRENTON

Thornton Wilder   one-act comedy

3m 3f   DPS

The parents and two children of an American family set out to visit their married daughter in Camden. Simply staged, Wilder's play examines the backbone of American culture and the family. Vivid scenes of the home and domestic life are interspersed with the dramatic character of the Mother. One of the characters is an author figure who stands and reads the parts of minor characters who never appear. A brilliantly simple and moving play.

HARD TIMES

Stephen Jeffreys, adapted from Dickens   drama

2m 2f   SF

A skillful adaptation of Dickens's novel about the Industrial Revolution. The play can be cast with either four actors playing all of the parts and sharing the narration, or it can be expanded to allow for each of the parts to be played separately. The set is likewise flexible, allowing for either simply staging or more elaborate sets, depending upon the group's needs.

HEARTBREAK HOUSE

Bernard Shaw   comedy

6m 4f   SF

One of Shaw's greatest plays, a brilliant comedy about Europe adrift from the past and tradition after the astonishing events of what came to be known as the the Great War. Memorable characters include Captain Shotover, Ellie Dunn, and Hesione Hushabye.

HERE AND NOW

David Rogers   drama

6m 7f & 3 extras   Dramatic

An unusual and thought-provoking play that brings together teenagers, parents, and teachers in an understanding that they are not alone in facing the pressures and confusions of contemporary adolescence. Staged in a bare high school auditorium, the play begins with the actors rehearsing a play loosely based on experimental sessions in which parents and teachers meet with teens to discuss human relations. Eventually the actors begin identifying with the parts they play and everyone, actors and audience alike, comes to a final understanding.

HIGH TIDE

Brad Slaight   **one-act comedy/drama**

3m 3f   **Bakers**

Two teens try to deal with the death of a friend. The older of the two boys knows that it was not an accidental death, but suicide. He cannot, however, bring himself to reveal this information to his friend. He confides in a stranger—a girl that he meets on the beach. The play deals with the issues of secrets to be kept and secrets to be told.

THE HOLLOW CROWN

John Barton   **"an entertainment"**

3m 1f   **SF**

An entertaining way to learn the history of England's Kings and Queens. The format is simple and elegant: Four actors play the parts of the monarchs, reciting letters, poems, and speeches, while three singers present music from the ages, some of which are about the death of kings, some of which are touching, and others that are funny.

HOMEROOM

Andrea Green & Selma Tolins-Kaufman   **musical**

8m 6f   **SF**

A wonderful opportunity for student groups to perform material that pertains to their own lives. This play runs the gamut from issues such as personal crises to school discipline, from the jocks to students with learning disabilities. As the musical progresses each student discovers that he or she does, in fact, have many of the same hopes and fears as the person sitting next to him or her in homeroom.

THE HOUSE OF BERNARDA ALBA

Federico Garcia Lorca   drama

10f, extras   SF

A translation of one of the great modern Spanish tragedies. It begins with the wid-
owing of Bernarda Alba who decides to enter the traditional eight years of clois-
tered mourning. Although her five daughters desire affection and compassion,
they each turn to their own secluded lives—all except one who engages in an
affair. As the play comes to its relentless end, the suitor is revealed to be the eldest
daughter's betrothed.

THE HOUSE OF RAMON INGLESIA

Jose Rivera   drama

5m 2f   SF

A probing drama about a brilliant young American's attempt to escape from his
immigrant parents. This play examines the necessity of exploring ones's ethnic
heritage as part of attaining a true sense of self. The play focuses on the daily lives
of the Inglesias, but this is more than a Hispanic play; it is a play about finding
identity in the uniquely American experience.

HOW TO EAT LIKE A CHILD

Delia Ephron, John Forster, & Judith Kahan   one-act musical

6-30 mix   SF

A musical revue about the joys and sorrows of childhood. The actors take the
audience through a series of lessons that are both funny and true; some include
"How to Stay Home from School" and "How to Beg for a Dog." Extremely flexible casting, from six to thirty actors can be used. This musical is as entertaining
as it is instructional.

HOW QUETZACOATL FOUND THE SUN

L.E. McCullough   one-act

14 chorus   S&K

From the rich traditions of the Aztecs comes a play based on one of the primary
creation myths of the Americas. Quetzacoatl was the serpent-god of the Aztecs,

and this short play details his struggle to help the world of men learn the gift of agriculture, while he battles the age-old enemies of the gods, the Tezcatlipocas, who wish to destroy the universe.

THE HUMAN COMEDY
William Dumaresq   **folk opera**
12m 10f   **SF**
A folk-opera about life in small town America during the early days of World War II. This play is about life, death, and growing up in a small community. The music emphasizes the feelings of love and courage that are woven throughout the play. Based on the novel by William Saroyan.

I

I HATE HAMLET
Paul Rudnick   **comedy**
3m 3f   **DPS**

Andrew Rally might seem to have the perfect actor's life: a hit TV series, a devoted agent, a beautiful girlfriend, and the perfect apartment. We find out, however, that the series is cancelled, the girlfriend refuses to give up her virginity, and the apartment is haunted by the agent's ex-flame, the departed Hamlet-extraordinaire, John Barrymore. Soon Andrew wrestles with choosing the right path, whether to play Hamlet, how to deal with a drunken ghost, and whether or not to escape to L.A. for a new series. Nonstop laughs make this bright comedy a sure audience pleaser.

I NEVER SAW ANOTHER BUTTERFLY
Celeste Raspanti   **drama**
4m 7f   **Dramatic**

The touching story of one woman's quest to keep hope and beauty alive in the Nazi concentration camps. Raja is the young Jewish teacher who teaches the children about love and laughter amidst the horror of Terezin. Butterflies come to represent the hope and defiance that she taught them, a lesson that helped them to survive or at least live in dignity. Also available in a one-act version.

I'M A FOOL
Sherwood Anderson, adapt. by Christopher Sergel   **one-act comedy**
4m 4f   **Dramatic**

Based on the story by Sherwood Anderson, *I'm a Fool* is the story of a poor stable hand who pretends to be a wealthy horse owner in order to win the love of the most beautiful girl that he has ever met. A tried and true adaptation of the original TV production starring James Dean that has won many high school contests.

I'M A STRANGER HERE MYSELF

Ev Miller   **drama**

6m 6f   **Dramatic**

Casey O'Hara is the good-looking high school guy who, in his senior year of high school, knows what he wants and where he is going. When his parents suddenly break up, however, Casey is forced to re-evaluate his choices, including his friendship with Mark Lee. When he meets a young girl, Lori, those choices seem even more precarious. Realistically and sensitively written, a wonderful choice.

THE IDIOT

David Fishelson   **drama**

9m 6f   **DPS**

A powerful drama based on the novel by Dostoyevski. The story is about Myshkin, a young man who returns to his home town after spending his youth being treated for epilepsy. His natural goodness and honesty bewitch all who meet him, including two beautiful women. Nastasya and Aglaya who, to his horror, fight for him before his very eyes. In the tragic conclusion, this play reveals how greed and lust can destroy the remaining goodness in human life.

IN A NORTHERN LANDSCAPE

Timothy Mason   **drama**

7m, 2f   **ICM**

In a Northern Landscape is Timothy Mason's haunting play of the incestuous relationship between a brother and sister in Minnesota in the 1920s. Drawn together by the boredom and isolation of their small farming community, their need for love leads to a tragic event that will leave Emma—the sister—and her family, with a lifetime of retribution and regret.

IN SIGHT

Louisville's Young Playwrights   **drama**

variable   **Dramatic**

Written by the young playwrights of Walden Theatre, this play is divided into two parts whose short pieces get to the heart of the joys, sorrows, and pressing issues that these young people see around them. Perfectly suited to young performers, with the ability to captivate young audiences as well, this play is a refreshingly honest celebration of today's youth.

INHERIT THE WIND
Jerome Lawrence & Robert E. Lee   drama
23m 7f   DPS
This play is based on the famous Scopes trial and brings to life all of the drama and passion of that time. It is an expressive portrait of a crucial moment in American culture, truly one of the best dramas of our times.

THE INNER CIRCLE
Patricia Loughrey   one-act drama
2m 2f   SF
The Inner Circle is the the story of Mark, a teenager who tried drugs once sharing the needle with a friend. Now Mark has AIDS, partly because he had no idea how the AIDS virus was transmitted. As he and his friends build a time capsule of memories by which they can hold onto Mark, we learn both about the celebration of life and friendship and about the tragedy of AIDS. The script includes up-to-date information on AIDS and HIV—an innovative and powerful project.

THE INNOCENTS
William Archibald   melodrama
1m 3f 1boy 1 girl   SF
Adapted from Henry James's horrifying novella, *The Turn of the Screw,* this play is the story of a young governess and her time with two young children. Soon she finds that the house is haunted by the ghosts of the former caretaker and maid who had corrupted the souls of the innocent young children. She is forced to recognize that the evil cannot be separated from innocence. This is a terrifying play that will hold audiences spellbound.

THE INSANITY OF MARY GIRARD

Lanie Robertson   **drama**

3m 4f   **SF**

When a young wife becomes pregnant by a man who is not her husband, the spurned husband has her locked away in an asylum, declared legally insane. Throughout the play, the Furies dance around her, re-enacting scenes and characters from her past. In the end, without choices, Mary Girard does finally go insane. A haunting piece.

INSIDE AL

David S. Baker   **one-act drama**

3m 2f   **SF**

A play about a group of high school kids who have been urged to take on a project—helping out someone in the community. They decide to help Al, a thirty-nine-year-old cerebral palsy victim who is both the man everyone sees, and the Al who wants to be a dancer—who is bitter and perceptive. This play has won several awards and is perfect for a high school production.

INSIDE OUT—UPSIDE DOWN

Walden Theater   **drama**

3m 3f (more possible)   **Dramatic**

A perceptive play about the barrier separating the physically handicapped from the non-handicapped. It deals with discrimination, prejudice, frustration, and misunderstanding—examining both sides of the barrier and eventually showing how we can all overcome our preconceived ideas and enter a world of understanding, appreciation, and even love.

INVISIBLE FRIENDS

Alan Ayckbourn   **fantasy**

4m 3f   **SF**

A play ostensibly for children but appealing to adults as well. It is the story of Lucy, a normal teenager who feels neglected by her parents. Lucy invents an invisible friend who comes to tea with her idealized family. The new family shows her how to make her family disappear, and life is wonderful until the truth about her new family is revealed. Simultaneously funny and serious with appeal for all ages.

IPHEGIA IN TAURUS
Euripedes, trans. Bynner   **drama**
4m 6f   **U of C**

Because later Greeks shied away from tales of human sacrifice, the story of Iphegia's sacrifice by her own father to ensure good winds to Troy was changed: Iphegia was carried away to Taurus by Artemis and becomes a priestess of her temple there. It is in Taurus that Iphegia finds herself reunited with her haunted brother Orestes, still seeking peace after the killing of his mother.

IT HAPPENS EVERY SUMMER
David Rogers   **comedy**
7m 13f   **Dramatic**

It Happens Every Summer is about a group of college girls who work as guest editors for a New York fashion magazine. In June, the editor-in-chief invites the winners of the Guest-Editor contest to New York. This year's winners prove to be a stranger group then ever: Jennifer, who desperately wants to work for the magazine; a gold-digging Southern belle; and an ambitious young writer looking for a publisher. Provides a highly comedic evening for all.

J

JABBERWOCK

Jerome Lawrence & Robert E. Lee   **comedy**

26m 17f   **SF**

The zany world of the Thurber family, as told by James Thurber. Witty, comical, often bittersweet, this play's crazy action includes Mrs. Thurber dressing up as a ghost to scare away a maid she can't bear to fire and the young James waking the family up at 3 AM to help him recall a bit of trivia. A wonderfully humorous evening is in store for audiences of the *Jabberwock*.

JANE EYRE

Helen Jerome   **drama**

10m 12f   **SF**

A dramatic, though slightly condensed version of Charlotte Brontë's classic eighteenth-century novel. Jane Eyre, a poor orphaned girl, comes to Thornfield as the governess for Adele, the ward of Mr. Rochester. Soon Jane and Rochester come to love each other; but when Jane discovers Rochester's still-living, though crazy, wife, she leaves Thornfield. A happy ending awaits Jane's trials.

JENNY KISSED ME

Jean Kerr   **comedy**

4m 10f   **DPS**

A young girl comes to live in the house of a priest, who soon finds himself engaged in trying to help make Jenny more attractive to the young men of the town. Various boys and girls help the priest in his endeavor. But Jenny finally picks the man who she has loved from the start, remaining throughout the play the simple charming young girl she always was. A widely popular play, funny and tender.

JOE TURNER'S COME AND GONE

August Wilson   drama
6m, 5f   SF

Another major work of American drama by August Wilson, who has so brilliantly chronicled the lives of dispossessed Black Americans in his plays, *Ma Rainey's Black Bottom* and *Fences*. This play centers around a Black boardinghouse where each resident manifests a distinct relationship to the history of slavery in America as well as to the urban present. Characters include the husband and wife who own the house, an eccentric man, a newly arrived Southern boy, and the mysterious man who says he is looking for his wife.

JOHN BROWN'S BODY

Stephen Vincent Benét   dramatic reading
3 speaking parts, chorus   DPS

An adaptation of Stephen Vincent Benét's epic poem by the same name. It chronicles the events of the Civil War era, beginning with John Brown's attack on Harper's Ferry and ending with the close of the Civil War. Although more a dramatic reading than a play, the principal speaking parts and the chorus help weave the actions and passions of the characters into a spellbinding theatrical experience.

JOHNNY APPLESEED AND WILLIE CRABGRASS

L.E. McCullough   one-act
10m 8f   S&K

Based on the real life of John Chapman, who spent his life travelling the United States during the early nineteenth century planting apple trees. It incorporates folklore of the period, which created a mischievous cousin of Johnny's, Willie Crabgrass, who spent his life growing weeds. This play dramatizes an episode between the two rivals and is a fine lesson on the importance of taking care of the environment.

JOHNNY TREMAIN

Lola H & Coleman A. Jennings   **history**

13m 2f   **Dramatic**

Adapted from the historical fiction of Esther Forbes, this play is the story of a apprenticed silversmith, Johnny, who finds himself caught up in the turbulent events of the Boston Tea Party and the Battle of Lexington. Johnny finds himself involved with John Hancock, Samuel Adams, and Paul Revere. It is not only the story of the American Revolution, it is the story of a young boy's struggle to survive without family or home.

JUST ONE DAY

Eddie Kennedy   **one-act drama**

1m 2f   **Dramatic**

A highly acclaimed one-act drama that deals with the pressing problem of teenage pregnancy. The play begins with Emily and Mary obviously waiting for someone, the tension builds until Michael arrives. When Mary leaves, Emily has to tell him that she is pregnant, and the remaining action deals with the two young people as they must face the difficult questions that arise. A television adaptation of this play has received several honors and awards.

K

KALEIDOSCOPE

Ray Bradbury   **one-act drama**

7m (f)   **Dramatic**

A one-act drama by Ray Bradbury that poses the questions of life and its purpose and allows the characters and actors alike to face dilemmas of profound importance. The action takes place in outer space as a rocket ship is hit by a meteor, leaving its pilot connected to the other crew members by the tenuous link of the communicator. The play allows unlimited possibilities for the director as well as the actors.

KIDNAPPED IN LONDON

Timothy Mason   **short play**

11m 2 f   **ICM**

"There is no creature more full of yearning than a young girl or boy." Corin is a simple country boy who lives the happy life of a daydreaming shepherd. His parents take him to London and he is is enthralled by the players he sees in the streets. As often happened in Elizabethan London in the late 1590s, Corin is kidnapped by the theater company and forced to perform. Ironically, he plays the part of a young shepherd and is a wonderful success. He struggles with his dueling desires to escape and return to his family, and his love for performing.

KING MIDAS AND THE GOLDEN TOUCH

L.E. McCullough   **one-act**

4m 2f   **S&K**

The well-known tale of the ancient Phrygian ruler who allows his greed for wealth to overwhelm his need for anything else in his life. Based on the original myth preserved in Ovid's *Metamorphoses,* it tells the story of Midas, who is given a special gift by the gods: Whatever he touches turns to gold. But the gift turns out to be a special curse.

KUNI-LEML

Nahma Sandrow   **musical farce**

6m 2f   **SF**

A musical farce about two young lovers defying tradition in the form of the young heroine's arranged marriage to a man she despises. *Kuni-Leml* is a classic Yiddish farce that has universal, family appeal. Bright, fun, and easy to produce, this modern play is sure to please.

L

LADYHOUSE BLUES

Kevin O'Morrison   drama
5f   SF

The place is St. Louis and the time is 1919, just after the war has ended. Five women await the return of the family's men. Liz, the central character is a young, gutsy, widow faced with the financial need to sell the family farm. Her four daughters wait with her: One is dying of tuberculosis, another has married into a society family, the third is a blooming young activist, and the youngest is about to lose her innocence forever. This play dramatically highlights a watershed year in American history by delving into the psyches of the women who endured it.

LADY'S NOT FOR BURNING, THE

Christopher Fry   comedy
8m 3f   DPS

A fanciful, poetic comedy about a discharged soldier who tries to get himself hanged by declaring that he has committed murder. At the same time a young women is charged with witchcraft and sentenced to hanging. Thomas, the soldier, argues for the young girl and the Mayor, who is about to hold a wedding, agrees to wait. During the crazy wedding that follows, the bride runs away, the brothers fight over her, the young women becomes the guest of honor, and Thomas falls in love. Justice and love both prevail as the murder victim arrives at the wedding and Thomas runs away with his new love.

THE LARK

Jean Anouilh & Lillian Hellman   tragedy
19m 7f   DPS

The mesmerizing tale of Joan of Arc comes alive in this timeless drama about both a moment in history and the young girl who sacrificed her life for her country. The play chronicles the trial and life of Joan while escaping the confines of time and place to bring to the stage a story of heart-stopping beauty and triumph. A unique way of telling an already beautiful tale.

THE LATE GREAT ME
David Rogers   **drama**
10m 12f   **Dramatic**

A touching but unflinchingly honest look at a serious problem facing American teens—alcoholism. It is the story of Geri Peters, shy and insecure, who finds that she has attracted the best-looking guy in her school. She finds out that he has sensed a weakness in her that leads to her own alcoholism. Sensitive and humorous at times, this play offers keen insight into teenage drinking.

LAUNDRY AND BOURBON
James McClure   **one-act comedy**
3f   **DPS**

Originally conceived as a companion piece to *Lone Star*, *Laundry and Bourbon* is set on Roy and Elizabeth's home in Maynard, Texas. Elizabeth and her friend Hattie are folding laundry, watching television, and drinking bourbon. As the two trade well-known secrets of their small town, they are joined by Amy Lee who reveals that Roy has been seen around town with another woman. Although the tone changes to a bitter humor, Elizabeth's strength and her love for Roy emerge—she knows that he needs her and that she will be waiting for him to come home no matter what he does.

LAVENDER AND OLD LACE
Rose Warner   **comedy**
4m 6f   **SF**

Lavender and Old Lace is the story of a charming old widow living out her strange life in a small New England town. Miss Ainslee agrees to take charge of her neighbor's niece as a favor and soon a young reporter with failing vision comes to town and falls in love with the young woman, Ruth. Carl and Ruth become engaged, but when he loses his sight, Miss Ainslee steps forward to help him regain his eyesight—and reveals the reason she has chosen to live such a strange life.

LEGEND OF THE SEASONS

Pamela Gerke   one-act

min 11 / max 30 m&f   S&K

A young man takes a spirit journey to find enlightenment and completion of himself. After breaking a rule the Island Woman tells him, she disappears. With the help of an invisible coat, he finds her again in the month of April.

LEMON SKY

Lanford Wilson   play

4m 3f   DPS

Lanford Wilson's compelling drama about the alienation between a young man and his father. *Lemon Sky* is the story of Alan, seventeen, who comes to visit his father in California—the father who years earlier had abandoned Alan's mother for another woman. Alan finds that his father has started a new life, but his hopes for finding peace in his relationship with his father are shattered by the older man's inability to act honestly.

THE LESS THAN HUMAN CLUB

Timothy Mason   drama

4m 4f   WM

Timothy Mason's story of a young man, Davis Daniels, who tries to recreate a turbulent and important year of his life (1968) in order to find answers for the paths that have led to where he finds himself today. *The Less than Human Club* is a journey back into the complexities of relationships, the crisis of sexual identity, friendship, and the search for real purpose and meaning in life.

LETTICE AND LOVAGE

Peter Shaffer   comedy

2m 3f   SF

Lettice and Lovage is a play about the desire to awaken people to the dreariness of their own lives. Peter Shaffer, the author of *Equus* and *Amadeus,* brings us the story of Lettice Duffet, who is a historian so bored with the truth of the historical house in which she works that she begins to embellish the truth with romantic visions of medieval heroism. An inspector of the Preservation Trust, Lotte, soon fires Lettice in the name of preserving history, but the two women soon become friends in an effort to bring color into the lives of their fellow citizens.

A LIFE IN THE THEATRE

David Mamet   **comedy**

3m   **SF**

A Life in the Theatre is a comedy about acting. It is the story of Robert, a seasoned professional, and John, an eager young actor who has yet to really prove himself. The two rehearse scenes from various plays—melodrama to Chekhov—and their rehearsals are frequently broken up by mishaps peculiar to the stage. Eventually the roles of teacher and student are reversed in Mamet's comic masterpiece.

LIFE WITH MOTHER SUPERIOR

Jane Trahey & Anna Helen Reuter   **comedy**

2m 25f   **DPS**

Both a best-selling novel and a motion picture, *Life with Mother Superior* begins with the arrival of new students at St. Mark's Academy. St. Mark's is a good but strict all-girls Catholic school. The girls start trouble by giving false names, and their deeds get zanier and zanier as the play brings to life the basic goodness and humanity in the sisters, the students, and the formidable Mother Superior.

LILY DALE

Horton Foote   **play**

4m 3f   **DPS**

One of the works in Horton's nine-play cycle, *Lily Dale* continues the saga of the Robedaux family in early twentieth-century Texas. In this play, the young Horace visits his mother and his sister in Houston where they live with his stepfather. Here he finds that his stepfather resents him, while doting on his sister, Lily Dale. An untimely sickness keeps him in the house, an opportunity to renew his relationship with his sister and purge the memories of their deceased alcoholic father. In the end, Horace returns to Harrison, leaving a newly healed family and possessing the strength to deal with his uncertain future.

LITTLE ORPHAN ANGELA

Charles H. Randall   **musical melodrama**

4m 4f   **Dramatic**

A musical melodrama that really works; it will have the audience booing and hissing at the evil Ignatius B. Cutworthy and cheering the efforts of the dashing hero, Andy Hanson, as the two men vie for the love of the beautiful Angela Tilford. Irresistible musical score accompanies the fun.

LITTLE SHOP OF HORRORS

Howard Ashman & Alan Manken   **musical comedy**

5m 4f   **SF**

A musical comedy that audiences will be horrified to enjoy. *Little Shop of Horrors* is the story of the lowly florist's assistant, Seymour, who tries to feed the voracious appetite of the flesh-eating plant he cares for. Seymour tries to win the love of Audrey, whose sadomasochistic dentist boyfriend provides a tasty meal for the insatiable and growing plant. The songs will have everyone humming for days and the laughs don't stop in this wickedly funny musical hit.

LITTLE WOMEN

Marion De Forrest   **comedy**

5m 7f   **SF**

A dramatization of Louisa May Alcott's well-loved masterpiece. *Little Women* is the story of a mother's love, a father's wisdom, and the lives of their four young daughters: Meg, Jo, Amy, and the angelic Beth. A timeless story for all audiences.

LONE STAR

James McClure   **one-act comedy**

3m   **DPS**

Set in the cluttered backyard of a Texas small-town bar, *Lone Star* is the hilarious study of two Texas "good ole boys." Roy, a brawny, macho type and once the local high school hero, is back from Vietnam and trying to re-establish himself in the community; Ray, who worships his younger brother, listens as we discover that Roy cherishes three things above all: his country, his sexy young wife, and his

1959 pink Thunderbird. As the case of beer disappears, so do the underpinnings of Roy's world when he finds out that his brother has slept with his wife and demolished his Thunderbird.

THE LOTTERY
Shirley Jackson dram. by Brainerd Duffield one-act drama
8m 5f Dramatic

A disturbing and unusual play based on the short story by Shirley Jackson. This dramatization begins, like the story, with a gathering of people who have assembled for the lottery. The tension builds as each member tries to guess who it will be this time. Slowly the audience begins to suspect the nature of the lottery and as the play comes to its horrifying climax, the tension and thrill of the play carry into the last moving scenes.

LOVE, DEATH, AND THE PROM
Jon Jory comedy/drama
flexible Dramatic

Mini-plays collected into one evening of fascinating drama. From the creator of *University, Love, Death, and The Prom* is a series of three plays about Love, Death, and ending with the Prom. *Love* is both touching and humorous, *Death* comes in the shocking news of a teen suicide, and finally *The Prom* ends the series. This play helps bring the audience to understand and appreciate these moments in the lives of America's youth.

LOVE LACE
Robert Patrick drama
1m 1f author

A short dramatic play by Robert Patrick. Its stark staging and simple casting contain a powerful dialogue between a man and a woman who have come to a bare room and try to find themselves and each other within it. A thought-provoking showcase for two actors.

LOVERS

Brian Friel   comedy

3m 5f   Dramatic

Lovers is a play in two parts, *Winners* and *Losers*. The first part is about a pair of young lovers whose love scene is contrasted with the dispassionate commentators. The audience soon learns that the lovers will die, but the triumph of their love carries over into the next part where we see the comic tragedy of older lovers.

THE LOWER DEPTHS

Maxim Gorky   drama

12m 5f   SF

A translation of Maxim Gorky's greatest work. The characters represent the dregs of society who have gathered in a disreputable inn and who are presented with a moment of happiness before it is destroyed by their own violent tendencies. Characters include a thief, a prostitute, the proprietor, the alcoholic actor, and the whistler who brings their brief hope.

LU ANN HAMPTON LAVERTY OBERLANDER

Preston Jones   drama

8m, 3f   H&W

This comedy/drama by Preston Jones is one of the plays comprising the acclaimed *A Texas Trilogy*. Set in the small town of Bradleyville we meet the intriguing character of LuAnn, and her dreams. In three separate decades, the life of LuAnn is revealed through a series of interpersonal relationships that are at times poignant, tragic, and even comic.

LYDIE BREEZE

John Guare   play

4m 3f   DPS

The setting is a worn beach house on Nantucket, the time is 1895. *Lydie Breeze* follows the fate and fortune of a family haunted by tragedy and buoyed by hope. Characters include the patriarch of the family, Joshua Hickman; his daughter, Lydie; the eldest daughter, Gussie; and Jeremiah Grady, the son of the man who Hickman killed when he discovered that Grady's father was his wife's lover. This play examines the intertwining idealism and corruption of American society.

M

MACK AND MABEL

Michael Stewart, Jerry Herman   **musical**

10m 5f   **SF**

A memorable musical that is a saga of the silent film era. The narrator and protagonist is Mack Sennett, a legendary director of comedy who has closed his studio; he tells the story in retrospect, beginning with his decline with the advent of the talkies. He recounts his turbulent affair with his favorite actress, Mabel Normand—the woman he loved and never told. Mabel left him for another man and soon found herself caught up in a world of drugs that would kill her. A traditional musical that resonates with truth and reminiscence.

THE MAGENTA MOTH

John Patrick   **thriller**

3m 5f   **DPS**

A horrifying thriller set in a remote mountain lodge. There an aging anthropologist, Dr. Cassandra (Cassie), and her lifelong friend, Grace, who has come to stay so that Cassie can recover from the back injury that has confined her to a wheelchair. Grace's nephew comes to visit, as well as a trio of teenage girls who profess to be lost hikers. Soon the older women realize that the young girls are wanted for a series of ritual slayings. When the girls discover that the women know who they are, a long night of terror begins in which the two women have only their wits to keep them alive.

MAGGIE MAGALITA

Wendy Kesselman   **drama**

1m 3f   **SF**

Perfect for high school productions, *Maggie Magalita* is the story of a fourteen-year-old Hispanic girl living with her mother in New York City. Young Maggie tries desperately to fit into the American lifestyle with much success but at the price of ignoring her own heritage. The arrival of her grandmother upsets Maggie's attempts to ignore her native culture. During a dinner to which her

American boyfriend is invited, however, Maggie discovers something of great value, her own identity.

MAKIN' IT

Cynthia Mercati **comedy**

10m 13f **SF**

Makin' It is the candid and unflinchingly insightful look into how teenagers go through the process of makin' it in high school. With uncannily real characters who are always real yet never stereotypes, this comedy brings to the stage the fears of being unpopular, the dangers of peer pressure, and the sometimes well-meaning, sometimes narrow-minded adults who the characters must confront.

MAMBO MOUTH

Leguizamo **drama**

1m **Bantam**

In the opening pages of John Leguizamo's collection of one-man scenes, the author offers that "This book is for all the Latin people who have had a hard time holding on to a dream and just made do." Mr. Leguizamo's characters are often irreverent but always startlingly truthful in portraying the diverse dynamics of Hispanic machismo. Behind the hilarity is a unique voice that is both pointed and honest.

THE MAN IN THE GLASS BOOTH

Bernard Shaw **drama**

18m 3f **SF**

The story of a German Jew, a wealthy real estate operator who lives in New York, flaunting his life as a Jew. Although he carries a revolver in fear, when Israeli officers track him down as a Nazi officer, he meekly surrenders. In an emotional tirade he admits to all his crimes, behind the walls of his glass booth, but a woman who claims to have known him as a Jew comes and deprives him even of this mask. An enthralling and thought-provoking play.

THE MAN WHO LOST THE RIVER

Bernard Sabath   comedy/drama

5m 5f   Dramatic

The play opens on a sunny afternoon in 1910, Samuel Clemens seventy-fifth birthday approaches and a young publisher comes to the house in an attempt to convince him to write again. Clemens claims that his humor is gone, his creativity dried up, and that he awaits Halley's Comet to take him from this world. A mysterious young tramp appears, however, and through Clemens's increasing understanding of him, Clemens begins to change his mind. The arrival of the comet and two quite recognizable young boys, however, interrupts Clemens's plans.

MANDRAKE

Machiavelli, trans. Frederick May & Eric Bentley   drama

5m 5f   SF

Machiavelli's only play and an Italian classic, this stage version of the ribald comedy is the story of an aging man who attempts to cure his wife's sterility but who is instead cuckolded by the fake doctor.

MARCUS BRUTUS

Paul Foster   dramatic tragedy

9m 4f   SF

A dramatic tragedy that has received enormous acclaim, *Marcus Brutus* plays with the intellectual metaphor of political murder and is structured as a psychological thriller. The characters of Caesar and Brutus come to life in the study of the playwright to re-enact the bloody events of a fight for power and political sovereignty. Laced with moments of comedy, the tension of impending drama builds throughout. A truly amazing play.

THE MASK

Dorothy R. Murphree   one-act drama

2m 2f   Dramatic

A dramatic presentation of the struggle undertaken by today's youth—the struggle for expression. Four characters put on masks in order to discuss their true feelings about each other, about war and the draft, about love and relationships, and about what they really want from life. The masks offer a way in which they can express themselves but also represent the impasse of honest expression in today's society.

MASTER HAROLD...AND THE BOYS

Athol Fugard   drama

3m (1 white, 2 black)   SF

Master Harold...and the Boys is the story of Hallie, a young white student who, engulfed in emotional turmoil, has made the perhaps irreversible step from childhood innocence to vicious bigotry. This change is reflected in his relationship with two boyhood friends, Sam and Willie, who work for Hallie's family in their tearoom. Set in South Africa, the play charts the deterioration of the friendship between the young men yet still maintains the optimism of reconciliation in the generous character of Sam.

MATAORA AND NIWAREKA IN THE UNDERWORLD

Pamela Gerke   one-act

min 8 / max 25 m&f   S&K

From the down-under-world of Australia, this Maori myth explains how certain things came to be: the Maori warrior tattoo called the moko, the beautiful designs and colors of Maori clothing, how popola (owl) and peka (bat) who can see in the dark came to live with us, and how the value of peace and gentleness was brought into the Overworld land of the living, from Rarohenga, the Underworld.

THE MATCHMAKER

Thorton Wilder   comedy

9m 7f   SF

Wilder's play is set in New York in 1880. There an aging merchant decides that he has accumulated enough wealth to take a wife and hires a matchmaker to find him one. The fast-paced farce soon has the merchant, the matchmaker, his clerks, and assorted young men and ladies running around trying to sort out their hearts. When this hilarious comedy comes to an end, everyone has his or her own heart's desire, and the merchant finds himself affianced to the astute matchmaker.

THE MATSUYAMA MIRROR

Velina Hasu Houston   one-act

1m 8f   H&CA

Set in Matsuyama Japan in the 1660s, *The Matsuyama Mirror* is the story of twelve-year-old Aiko and her wealthy Japanese family. It is based on an ancient Japanese fairy tale. Young Aiko loses her mother whom she was very close to, and her father brings her the gift of a mirror that allows her to see her mother as a young girl—reflected in the glass is Aiko's own face. When her father marries her mother's sister, young Aiko must face her own grief as well as the changes within her body. Written specifically for young actors, a superb short play.

ME AND MY GIRL

L. Arthur Rose, Dougla sFurber, & Noel Gay   musical

11m 8f   SF

A musical comedy with a simple yet engrossing plot, *Me and My Girl* is the story of the late Viscount Hereford's long lost (or rather hidden) son and heir. Bill Snibson moves into the ancestral hall to the horror of the aristocracy. The upper crust soon is converted by the antics of Bill, his girl Sally, and all of his mates who have piled into Hereford to claim his birthright.

THE ME NOBODY KNOWS

Robert Livingston & Herb Schapiro   musical

12 total   SF

What began as a collection of writings of ghetto children—their reflections, hopes, and dreams—has been transformed into a stunning theatrical event with the addition of a semi-rock musical score. This play tackles such issues as the slums, poverty, drugs, school, as well as more fanciful issues. The teenage characters sing and dance their way into the hearts of the audience with their striking individuality and heart-warming hope.

MEDEA

Euripides   **tragedy**

5m 2f   **public domain**

A classic Greek tragedy, Euripedes' *Medea* is the story of a woman forsaken and rejected by her husband, the hero, Jason. Medea, the foreign wife who helped Jason on his journey, is rejected by him in his homeland; as revenge, Medea kills her own children.

MERRILY WE ROLL ALONG

Sondheim & Furth   **musical**

27 mix   **SF**

Based on the original play by George Kaufman and Moss Hart. This fun musical runs backwards! Each scene is set a few years earlier than the one before it. The audience is required to participate by remembering odd and obscure references until the answers reveal themselves. A fun ride!

THE MIDNIGHT CALLER

Horton Foote   **one-act drama**

2m 5f   **DPS**

The Midnight Caller is set in a boardinghouse in a small Texas town, near the coast. Living in the house are three, unmarried women: Alma Jean, Miss Rowena, and Cutie, who have sat and watched the lives of the townspeople for years. A young women, Helen Crews, comes to live with them after a disagreement with her mother. Helen had been engaged to Harvey Weems, but the two mothers manage to break up the engagement. Charming, though weak, Harvey comes to see Helen every night, calling up to her window. Another young man, the attractive Ralph Johnston, moves into the boardinghouse and manages to help Helen move on to a new life and love, leaving the midnight caller alone at her window.

A MIDSUMMER NIGHT'S DREAM

William Shakespeare   **comedy**

13m 7f   **public domain**

In this comedy about the transition from adolescence to adulthood, two couples enter the woods on a midsummer night. Two of the youths are in love with the same girl. The fairies try to remedy this, but through a series of mistakes and love potions, the relationships become even more confused. The characters are not particularly distinctive from each other. Their relationships are paralleled by the adolescent relationship between the fairy king and queen and the mature relationship between the king of Thebes and his bride.

THE MIKADO
Gilbert & Sullivan   **musical**
flexible   **SF**
Gilbert and Sullivan's most popular operetta. Set in medieval Japan, the plot deals with mistaken identity, romance, and the foibles of politics. The main characters include The Mikado, Koko, Pooh Bah, Yum Yum, and Katisha the middle-aged daughter-in-law elect. Fast paced, lively, and entertaining.

MINNIE'S BOYS
Arthur Marx & Robert Fisher   **musical**
1f mix   **SF**
A romping musical based on the lives of the Marx Brothers. This musical is the touching celebration of a show-business legend, Minnie Marx. She is the woman who gave birth to the laughter of millions in the form of her five sons. This play is their story, but it is also their mother's story. Rousing songs will have audiences singing and smiling.

A MINUET
Louis N. Parker   **one-act poetic drama**
2m 1f   **SF**
A poetic drama set in the time of the French Revolution. A French aristocrat and his estranged wife are reunited in a touching scene as they await their execution on the guillotine. Written in verse, this play examines the moral courage and innate nobility manifested by certain French aristocrats in an era of terror and upheaval. A perfect play to showcase high school talent.

THE MIRACLE WORKER
William Gibson   drama
7m 7f   SF

A stirring dramatization of Helen Keller's life story. The play focuses on the relationship between Annie Sullivan, the blind Irish woman who saw the strong mind
and character of a girl trapped in a world of darkness and isolation. The final real-
ization of Helen's character and culmination of the emotional relationship
between the two women comes only after several violent and emotional scenes.

THE MISS FIRECRACKER CONTEST
Beth Henley   comedy
2m 4f   DPS

In the small Mississippi town of Brookhaven, a few days before the Fourth of July,
Carnelle Scott rehearses furiously for the Miss Firecracker Contest, hoping that
victory will salvage her tarnished reputation (she is known locally as Miss Hot
Tamale). The arrival of her cousin Elaine—a former Miss Firecracker, who has left
her rich husband and an unhappy marriage—and the repeated threats of her eccentric brother, Delmount, complicate her aspirations. With the help of her cousin
and the awkward seamstress in love with her brother, Carnelle perseveres. A triumphant ending with hope of a new and better life.

MISTER MAGISTER
Thomas F. Monteleone   one-act drama
5m 1f   WM

A morality play in one act, in the tradition of *The Twilight Zone.* Winner of The
Gabriel Award, and the Bronze Award, at the New York Television and Film
Festival. A nameless small town is visited by a lone carnival wagon, The
Magnificent Gallery of Mister Magister. It is a shooting gallery that attracts the
business of everyone in the town. But the longer the gallery remains popular, the
more unexplained deaths occur within the community. The connection between
the strange visitor and what is happening to the people in the town is finally
revealed through the efforts of Stella, a teenage girl.

MIXED BABIES

Oni Faida Lampley   drama

5f   DPS

Mixed Babies is the story of a search for identity and womanhood. Set in Oklahoma City in the mid 1970s, the play focuses on Reva and a group of her friends who are having a slumber party. Each of the five girls is in the process of discovering herself in terms of their racial identity in America. Reva hopes to embrace her African heritage by undergoing a Rite of Passage; although reluctant, her friends agree to help her. In the end, each of the girls has discovered something about themselves and about who they want to be.

MOBY DICK REHEARSED

Orson Welles, from Herman Melville   melodrama

12m 2f   SF

Welles's ingenious adaptation of Melville's classic story. The play opens with a Shakespearean Company that stops its rehearsal of *Lear* and takes up a new play, *Moby Dick*. Soon the stage becomes the ship, *Pequod,* and the cast sets sail through the trials of the adventure that is *Moby Dick*.

THE MONKEY KING

L.E. McCullough   one-act

3m 2f chorus   S&K

This play is adapted from one of stories from the collected parables by Siddhartha Gautama, also known as Buddha. As founder of the Buddhist religion, he became famous for his teachings of love and nonviolence, and the notion of reincarnation. This play tells the story of the king of the monkeys whose love of his kind is ultimately proved by his sacrificing his life to teach them the value of love and respect.

THE MONKEY'S PAW

W. W. Jacobs & Louis N. Parker   one-act thriller

4m 1f   SF

The Whites have a visitor, Major Morris; the Major has with him a monkey's paw and he tells them that it has the power to grant three wishes. The Major warns them that the paw has brought only grief to those who use it, but Mr. White accepts it and wishes for $200. Soon the Whites learn that their son has been killed at work but as compensation the company is giving them $200! Next Mr. White wishes for his son to be restored to life. A knock on the door is heard but before the distraught mother can open it, Mr. White wishes that his son may return to the grave.

MOON OVER THE BREWERY

Bruce Graham drama

2m 2f DPS

Moon over the Brewery is the story of a brilliant young girl, Amanda, and her single mother who supports them by waitressing. The lonely mother's passion is for her painting, but the bleak Pennslyvania landscape affords little in the way of subjects; she dons a miner's hat and goes out at night to paint by the soft moonlight. Meanwhile, Amanda has managed to drive away all of her mother's suitors with barbed comments; to fulfill her own need for male companionship, Amanda has created an imaginary friend, Randolph. It is finally the unlikely person of Warren the mailman who manages to beat Amanda at her own game and banish Randolph into the fantasy world where he belongs.

THE MOST DANGEROUS WOMAN IN AMERICA

L.E. McCullough one-act

7m 7f S&K

A riveting and revealing play about a little-known hero of the American labor-movement, Mary Harris Jones, better known as Mother Jones. Set in the present, a fast-food restaurant is visited by a mysterious old woman, who educates the people there on the history of labor in a time when workers were not organized or protected. Through flashbacks, we see episodes that depict the struggles of workers to achieve fair treatment.

MOST VALUABLE PLAYER

Mary Hall Surface drama

12m 5f CTC

Most Valuable Player, the highly-acclaimed play about Jackie Robinson's struggles with human rights and social equality, and his courageous breakthrough into major league baseball.

MOTHER HICKS
Susan L. Zeder   **drama**
1m 2f chorus   **Dramatic**
There's witchcraft in the air as a young and homeless girl in the darkest years of the Depression meets the indomitable title character and her friend, an eloquent deaf man named Tuc. The witch stories, including the locations and details of place and period, are historically accurate.

MOTHERS AND DAUGHTERS
Mario Fratti   **mystery**
2m 4f   **SF**
A psychological thriller, *Mothers and Daughters* is a mystery in which a wealthy family home is the site of a horrible crime. No murder has been committed and no detective has been called, but the crime has happened. Someone has been the victim of a cruel crime. Is the mother responsible? Reversals and discoveries keep the audience on the edge of their seats and the ending promises to startle everyone.

MR. SCROOGE
Richard Morris, Dolores Claman & Ted Wood   **Christmas musical**
10m 9f, 4 ghosts, extras   **Dramatic**
The Christmas musical based on Charles Dickens's beloved novel. The catchy music adds an unexpected and enriching element to the well-known story of Ebenezer Scrooge and the visitations of the three ghosts. As the ghosts reveal elements about his true nature, Scrooge is shocked into helping the poor but happy family of his employee, Bob Cratchet.

MS. SCROOGE

P. M. Clepper   **Christmas**

22f   **Dramatic**

A new twist to an old story. Ms. Scrooge changes the characters from Ebenezer to
Edna, from Bob Cratchet to Bobbie Cratchet, and from Tiny Tim to Little Liza.
The change from male to female characters adds a whole new element, while the
story and the moral it contains remains intact.

MURDER TAKES THE VEIL

Margaret Ann   **mystery**

8m 15f   **Dramatic**

Set in a convent school, this thriller is an exciting mystery in an unexpected setting. It is the story of Trillium, a young student who finds an article that belonged
to her dead father. She realizes that she is in trouble when another student, wear-
ing an identical costume for the school play, is found murdered. Who is the killer
and what might he be trying to hide?

MUSEUM

Tina Howe   **comedy**

9m 9f   **SF**

Museum is set on the final day of an art show featuring the work of three fictional,
contemporary American artists. It takes place in a major museum of modern art
and reveals the thoughts and yearnings of the forty or so people who walk through
the exhibit. From art lovers to critics, students to fellow artists, lost souls to
museum guards, we are given an intimate look into the lives of these people
through the medium of art.

MUSICAL COMEDY MURDERS OF 1940

John Bishop   **comedy**

5m 5f   **DPS**

The creative team responsible for a recent Broadway flop, unhelped by the murder
of three showgirls by the infamous Stage Door Slasher, come together for a
backer's audition of their new show. The house in which they perform has every-

thing from sliding secret doors to a German maid who seems to be three people. The comic mayhem that ensues comes from the arrival of a blizzard cutting off escape and the appearance of the Slasher who strikes again and again. A wonderfully witty farce that pokes fun at just about everything in "show biz."

MY CHILDREN! MY AFRICA!
Athol Fugard   **drama**
2m 1f   **SF**
Inspired by a true incident in South Africa, this is the story of one soul who truly believed in the power of the pen over violence. Mr. M. tries to teach and save one student, telling him that South Africa's problems can be solved through education not through violence; his white assistant, Isabel, also befriends the young man, Thami. Ultimately Thami is thrown toward the side of violence when Mr. M. admits that he has been an informer in an attempt to avoid violence. As Mr. M. is beaten to death, only Isabel remains to honor the humble man who tried to win through peace.

MY SISTER EILEEN
Joseph Fields & Jerome Chodorov   **comedy**
21m 6f   **DPS**
My Sister Eileen is the story of two young girls who have leased a basement apartment in Greenwich village. Eileen is the pretty one who attracts attention from every man who sees her; Ruth is plainer, and instead of having stage aspirations, she is absorbed in literature. The flow of characters in and out of the apartment is the source of this comedy's laughter.

MY SISTER IN THIS HOUSE
Wendy Kesselman   **drama**
4f   **SF**
This extraordinary drama has been produced to critical acclaim and debuted at the Actors Theatre of Louisville. *My Sister in This House* tells the story of an infamous French murder case in which two maids, who are sisters, kill the mother and daughter of the house in which they were employed. The play examines the

motives that led the sisters to murder and is a stunning look into the psychiatry of a murder.

THE MYSTERY OF IRMA VEP

Charles Ludlam   **comedy**

2m   **SF**

A Gothic melodrama in which only two actors play all of the roles. A truly vaudevillian mix of thrills, laughs, and pure showmanship, *The Mystery of Irma Vep* includes such characters as a sympathetic werewolf, a vampire, and an Egyptian princess who has been resurrected.

N

NE HOLMOLAISET (THE SILLY VILLAGER)

Pamela Gerke   one-act

min 7 / max 25 m&f   S&K

This play from Finland is presented as a set of three very silly stories: "The Sickle and the Sillies," "The Light and the Light-headed," and "Idiots on Ice." The Silly Villagers lived alone, never seeing or hearing anything of the outside world. They do things in their own silly way, and regard anything else as threatening and evil. This is too bad, as their silly ways of doing things are not very productive.

THE NERD

Larry Shue   comedy

5m 2f   DPS

One of the funniest plays on stage, *The Nerd* centers on a young architect, Willum Cubbart. Cubbart has often told his friends about how a another young man, Rick Steadman, saved his life in Vietnam. Although he never met Rick, Willum promised him that he would do anything for him. When the two men finally meet, the comedy heats up, for Rick Steadman proves to be a hopeless nerd with no social skills—and no desire to leave.

NEVER MIND WHAT HAPPENED, HOW DID IT END?

David Rogers   comedy

19m 19f (doubling possible)   Dramatic

A charming and dynamic play about three generations of love. Simultaneously contemporary and nostalgic, the play focuses on a young girl, Ann; her mother Donna; and her grandmother, a former movie star. The story reveals the three young girls in three different time periods, struggling with the joys and woes of young love. Cleverly interwoven, it offers an intriguing look into the romances of young people.

NICE PEOPLE DANCING TO GOOD COUNTRY MUSIC

Lee Blessing   **play**

3m 2f   **DPS**

The play involves two women, Eve Wilfong, and her niece, Catherine Empanger. Eve lives above a country music bar in Houston, and Catherine comes to live with her after having been asked to leave her convent because of a strange tendency to shout obscenities and even bark like a dog. A young man shows interest in Catherine, but the older Eve decides to give her the benefit of her own experience before letting her loose in the world of modern love. A charming comedy, both sharp and romantic.

THE NIGHTINGALE

Timothy Mason   **short play**

3m 3 f 6 mixed cast   **ICM**

Hans Christian Andersen's magical tale told here through narration, dance, costume, and movement. The Chinese emperor lives in a porcelain palace oblivious to the real treasures of his kingdom. He discovers the plain-looking nightingale, whose beautiful voice pleases him more than any of the beautiful things in his kingdom. He keeps the nightingale locked up, until the Japanese bring him a mechanical, jeweled bird and he forgets his friend. When the emperor grows sick and his mechanical bird breaks, the nightingale returns to sing for him and toward off death. The emperor learns the important lesson that one ought "not be in such a hurry to get there that you forget why you went."

NIGHTS IN HOHOKUS

Jason Milligan   **one-act comedy**

2m   **SF**

Manny and Lenny are two close friends, a little wild and crazy, who spend most of their time sitting around their favorite bar in Hohokus, New Jersey. Soon, Lenny, the younger of the two friends, decides that he should do something with his life and gets a job. Manny resents his friend's new life, saying he cannot hold a job because of an injury. A funny but poignant look at how friendships grow and change.

NO EXIT

Jean Paul Sartre   **drama**

2m 2f   **SF**

A thought-provoking fantasy about eternal torment. Two women and one man are locked up in Hell. There is one room, no windows or doors; there are no mirrors, and the lights can never be turned off. The torture of this Hell is not that of fire and brimstone, but that of the stripping humiliation of a soul bared to the world for all eternity.

NO PLACE TO BE SOMEBODY

Charles Gordone   **drama**

11m 5f   **SF**

A Black bar owner has a grand plan for making it big, but when his mentor is released from prison, he is disappointed to find that the older man is pacified, urging him to give up the fight against Charley. To make matters worse, the Mafia begins to give him trouble for being too ambitious. When he meets a young white girl parading for Black rights, he takes her to his home and heart, abandoning his Black girlfriend. As the new couple try to blackmail the Mafia using files stolen from her father—a judge, the play builds to a violent climax. A black and turbulent comedy.

NOAH

Andre Obey   **fantasy**

5m 4f   **SF**

A fantasy about the well-known plight of Noah. The voyage on the ark begins auspiciously with Noah, his family, and three neighborhood girls. The hope of a new world and the dawn of a new age fill them as the rains stop and they rejoice in the possibility of a clean start. Unfortunately, parts of the old world plague them; Ham, the younger son, taunts the others with fears from the old life. As Noah grows lonely in his faith but continues to guide the ship toward its destiny, we see the young people prepare to abandon the old man. An ideal play for advanced groups.

NOISES OFF
Michael Frayn   **farce**
5m 4f   **SF**

A farce of a farce, *Noises Off* has three acts: The first is a pastiche of traditional farce, the second a contemporary variant of the first, and the last act is an undermining of the entire genre. The action centers on a touring company during a dress rehearsal of a traditional farce, *Nothing On*. What follows from there is truly an original delight that mixes mockery with homage and includes all the comedic caricatures one could ask for.

THE NUTCRACKER
June Walker Rogers   **Christmas fantasy**
10m 12f   **Dramatic**

The beloved story of *The Nutcracker* in a play perfect for high school students. During a Christmas Eve party, Clara's grandfather presents her with a fascinating nutcracker, carved in the form of a toy soldier. When the nutcracker is brought to life, he tells her that he is a prince under the enchantment of the wicked Mouse King. Soon Clara finds herself helping through a series of fantastical adventures. When she awakens, the nutcracker is gone, but her grandfather returns with his nephew, a young man who looks exactly like the prince!

O

OF POEMS, YOUTH AND SPRING

John Logan   one-act comedy

1m 1f (3 voices, 4 chorus)   SF

About the first romance of a young high school couple. The play has four acts that correspond both to the seasons in which they take place and also to the actions that take place in them. Spring is when they meet, winter when they part. Two small choruses introduce each act, playing incidental roles in the play and providing stage assistance. The choruses provide contrast to the lighthearted comedy of the romance.

OKLAHOMA

Rodgers & Hammerstein   musical

1f. mixed   RHML

A timeless favorite, *Oklahoma* is a romantic musical that follows the nostalgic story of a handsome cowboy, a beautiful young girl, and the joys and trials of their courtship. Songs include: "Oh What a Beautiful Mornin'," "Kansas City," "I Can't Say No," and "People Will Say We're in Love."

OLIVER

Bart   musical

1m mixed   TW

Based upon Charles Dickens's novel, *Oliver Twist,* this musical follows the London boyhood of a young orphan who starts out in a workhouse and finds peace and love. During the course of his adventures, Oliver will fall prey to an infamous den of thieves who try to train him in their craft. The play contains a cast of memorable Dickensian characters and an equally memorable musical score.

ONCE A CATHOLIC

Mary O'Malley   comedy

4m 10f   SF

This brilliant comedy is based on the author's own experiences in a London convent. Although the title might imply the thought, "always a Catholic," this play reveals the perseverance of children in spite of, not because of, their education and indoctrination. Centering around Class 5A, in which all the girls except one Maria, are named Mary. The protagonist is a Mary referred to as Mooney, a young girl who has yet to learn the benign art of deception and thus is a perpetual scapegoat. Although the focus is on the various amusing ways in which the girls integrate the dogma being force-fed to them, a serious question about education lurks beneath the laughter.

ONCE IN A LIFETIME
George S. Kaufman & Moss Hart   **comedy**
24m 14f   **SF**
A romping tale of three down-on-their-luck troupers who head to Hollywood hoping to find success in the new "talkies" of the day. Due to a series of blunders, the most stupid of the three men finds himself thrust into stardom, becoming a literal god of the new industry. A marvelously funny spoof of tinsel town.

ONCE UPON A MATTRESS
Rogers, Thomson, & Miller   **musical**
1m mixed   **RHML**
A retelling of Hans Christian Andersen's *The Princess and the Pea*. All the original plot elements are funneled through the conventions of the American Broadway show.

ONCE UPON A SUMMERTIME
Mary W. Schaller   **one-act comedy**
1m 1f   **Dramatic**
A young girl, Tiffany Johnson, has been blinded in an auto accident and is sent to her grandparents' home in the north woods. Here she meets Robin, an unusual boy who is cheerful, musical, and impossibly irreverent. With his musical talent and refusal to be overly sympathetic, Robin manages to lure Tiffany back into the world where she learns to read Braille, play the flute, and eventually to accept and go beyond her blindness.

ONDINE

Jean Giraudoux, adp. Maurice Valency   fairy tale

17m 11f   SF

A tragedy about the incompatibility of dreams and reality. It is the romantic story of a beautiful young nymph who falls in love with a handsome knight. They are married in court, but they soon learn that their ideal love cannot survive the shocks of a cruel world. The knight dies of grief and the nymph returns to the perfect world from which she came.

ONE FLEW OVER THE CUCKOO'S NEST

Dale Wasserman   comedy/drama

13m 4f   SF

Adapted from the novel by Ken Kesey, *One Flew Over the Cuckoo's Nest* is the story of a charming young rogue who manages to get himself put into a state mental institution rather than serving a prison term for a minor offense. He soon shakes up the ward, encouraging the introverted inhabitants to come out of their silence. The head nurse and he soon become bitter enemies, a rivalry that ends in tragedy when he is forced to undergo a frontal lobotomy.

THE OPEN ROAD

Brad Slaight   short play

2m 1f   author

The Open Road is about the Sommers family: Amanda, the mother who leads the family is strong, sympathetic, and supportive; Jack, the father, a dreamer who has buckled down under the responsibility of a family; and Allen, the perfectly normal son who undergoes a radical change that will affect his entire life as well as his parents' lives. While Amanda feels that she is losing her husband and son to the wear and tear of the everyday, her son finds release in Whitman's poetry and eventually in his identity. This profound change causes his parents to rethink the direction of their lives.

ORDINARY PEOPLE

Judith Guest & Nancy Pahl Gilsenan   drama

6m 3f   Dramatic

Conrad Jarrett was the younger of two sons, but now his older brother, Buck, is gone. *Ordinary People* is the story of a family struggling to survive. The well-intentioned father, the remote and beautiful mother, and their friends are all in jeopardy and this play goes to the essence of the relationships and their struggle. An extraordinary opportunity for talented young actors to challenge themselves and each other.

ORPHANS

Lyle Kessler   comic drama

3m   SF

A stirring drama about a dying mother and the selfishness of her three children. The first daughter waits with her little girl and her brother to hear news of their dying mother. Together they berate each other and their absent sister, who proves to be even more selfish then they. The young child is slapped when their hysterical arguing causes her to cry. A policeman returns her after she runs away, telling them that their mother has died. But still the small girl is ignored in the new orphans' show of grief.

OUR MISS BROOKS

R. J. Mann   comedy

5m 12f   Dramatic

An oft-produced and always lauded play, *Our Miss Brooks* is the story of a teacher looking forward to a vacation. When she discusses her upcoming cruise with the school's athletic coach, Miss Brooks imagines that he is the man of her dreams. Soon, however, she finds herself in competition with him for the gym and for his players as she directs the school play. A wonderful comedy.

OUR TOWN

Thorton Wilder   drama

17m 7f   SF

Thorton Wilder's Pulitzer Prize–winning play *Our Town* is set in a small New

Hampshire town in 1901. George Gibbs and Emily Webb are childhood friends and neighbors. Their shy romantic interest in one another culminates in a marriage proposal over an ice cream soda. Their happiness is short-lived, however, as Emily dies. This play examines the mystery of death that cannot be understood by the living.

OUT OF GAS ON LOVERS LEAP

Mark St. Germain   **drama**

1m 1f   **DPS**

Myst and Grouper are two affluent and intelligent teenagers who have come to the local lovers leap for a private celebration. Myst is the daughter of an aging rock star with dubious morals, and Grouper is the son of an ambitious and egotistical Senator. While Myst is determined to make love to Grouper, he wants to wait until they are married. Soon a mixture of alcohol and drugs leads them to have sex, but it is an act as empty as the lives that their elders have allowed them to live. A terrible and heartrending ending completes the tragedy of these lost youths.

THE OUTSIDERS

S.E. Hinton   **drama**

10m 8f   **Dramatic**

Adapted from the novel by S.E. Hinton, *The Outsiders* is a play about real people, about young men and women growing up and finding themselves. It is the story of Sodapop, Bob, the sensitive Ponyboy, and Dallas. It centers on the rivalry between the Greasers, who have each other, and the Socs, who have everything else. A touching story of friendship that will always ring true.

AN OVERPRAISED SEASON

Richard S. Dunlop   **one-act play of ideas**

4m 2f   **SF**

An award-winning play that was designed for advanced student performers, *An Overpraised Season* is the powerful story of the myriad problems facing today's youth. In episodic form with a narrator, this forty-minute play involves two boys and one girl, a fanatically religious mother, and a selfish father.

P

PAINTED RAIN

one-act drama   **2m 1f**

author

Painted Rain is the touching story of two foster children, Dustin, a handicapped boy of sixteen, and Teddy an eleven-year-old boy. This short play focuses on the relationship between the older boy, a painter, and the soon-to-be-adopted Teddy.

PEER GYNT

Henrik Ibsen   **poetic fantasy**

26m 12f   **SF**

Henrik Ibsen's poetic fantasy of a young man, Peer Gynt, who is a wild and imaginative lad. He runs off with a young bride disappointed in her marriage, but eventually deserts her and becomes an outcast. He comes to live with the pagan spirits of the woods, who share his understanding of the world but whose wantonness and ugliness drive him away. At the end of his life, Peer Gynt realizes that no one can live alone, and he is thrown back into the melting pot of humanity to be molded again.

THE PEOPLE NEXT DOOR

JP Miller   **drama**

5m 3f   **DPS**

A powerfully dramatic play about teenage drug abuse and the generation gap. The story centers around two seemingly perfect suburban families: In one the sixteen-year-old daughter becomes addicted to LSD, and in the other the son is revealed to be nothing better than a pusher bent on making money by selling drugs to his peers. The play traces the path of destruction, the failed attempts at therapy, and finally the tragedy whose only redemption is the hope that it may teach others.

PERFECT CRIME

Warren Manzi   thriller

1f 4m   SF

A spine-tingling cat-and-mouse thriller about a woman psychiatrist and her husband, also a psychiatrist, who return to America, settling in Windsor Locks,
Connecticut. In this small town at least one murder has already been committed
and the local cop, obsessed with the crime as well as Margaret Thorne Brent and
her patients, sets out to solve the mystery.

PETER PAN

J. M. Barrie   fantasy

25, mix   SF

Available in several versions of varying length and cast size, *Peter Pan* offers a magical fantasy to actors and audience members alike. It is the irresistible tale of Peter
Pan, the fairy Tinker Bell, and the young children who follow them into Never-
Never Land where no one grows old but where Captain Hook and his pirates are
still to be feared.

PHANTOM OF THE OPERA

Joseph Robinette   musical

6m 4f, flexible chorus   Dramatic

The enchanting musical based in Gaston Leroux's classic love story, *Phantom of
the Opera* captures all of the romance and mystery of nineteenth-century France.
It is the story of the young singer, Christine; her suitor, Raoul; and the "Opera
Ghost." A versatile score with many great parts in addition to the three principal
actors, this version of *Phantom* offers a challenging but rewarding theater experience.

PHILADELPHIA STORY

Philip Barry   comedy

9m 6f   SF

The romantic comedy about a rather cold Philadelphia socialite, Tracy Lord, and
her wedding to a smug and successful snob, Kittredge. Tracy was formerly mar-

ried to C. K. Dexter Haven who arrives at her wedding along with a reporter and his photographer. The two have been brought to the house in an attempt to divert attention from Tracy's father's dalliance with a Broadway dancer. Soon Tracy is drawn to the dashing reporter; the result of which is a refusal to marry Kittredge and a reunion with her real love, Dexter Haven.

PICNIC AT HANGING ROCK

Laura Annawyn Shamas   **mystery**
8m 18f   **Dramatic**

A murder mystery based on the book by Joan Lindsay. Three seniors and their math teacher have disappeared from the top of the jagged peaks of Hanging Rock. Who is responsible for this crime? Miss Appleyard, the headmistress who drinks brandy on the sly? the beautiful French teacher? or one of the eight remaining girls? This play explores the effects of this baffling disappearance on a small Australian town and looks into crisis, greed, and honesty at the turn of the century.

THE PIGMAN

Paul Zindel   **play**
6m 3f   **DPS**

Adapted from the novel by Paul Zindel, *The Pigman* is the story of the relationship between two young teenagers, Lorraine and John. Bored with their lives, the pair search for other activities to fill their time. During one such activity, conceived as a scam by which to obtain money from an unsuspecting donor, the two meet Mr. Pignati. Mr. Pignati is a retired widower who collects pigs; and as the two are drawn into his life, the play unfolds a series of scenes with the Pigman and with their parents. Looking closer and closer into the heart of their developing relationship with him, this play moves inexorably toward tragedy.

PINOCCHIO

Timothy Mason   **short play**
6m 3f, 4 m&f   **ICM**

An Italian tale of a little wooden puppet that wants to be a real boy. Pinocchio must learn the ways of the world and earn boyhood through good behavior. He has the help of his father, Gepetto the wood carver, and the benevolence of the Blue Fairy. This doesn't stop him from getting into trouble, being tempted by fame and fortune, and swindled by con men. His love for his father and his desire to be a real boy see him through and save him in the end.

PIPPIN
Schwarz & O'Hirson   **musical**
11m 3f   **MT1**
Book by Roger O. Hirson with music and lyrics by Stephen Schwartz. Costume drama with music; the son of Charlemagne as the lead character. The plot deals with a young man's journey to find complete fulfillment and meaning in his life. Either disappointed or thwarted by his every attempt to understand the truth, his mistakes are compounded through time until he learns, too late, that his ultimate goal will always elude him.

PLACES, PLEASE
Herb Martin   **musical**
6m 6f, flexible chorus   **Dramatic**
A young high school student, Colin, has written a new musical based on Dickens's *David Copperfield*. Auditions are in the works for the play that is to be performed by the senior class, but no one has prepared either Colin or the sympathetic teachers for the effect that competition will have on the students' personal relationships. A delicate and insightful look both into the magic of behind-the-scenes action and into what is really important to these young people. The musical-within-a-musical form allows for a wide variety of songs.

PLAIN AND FANCY
Joseph Stein & William Glickman   **musical**
19m 11f   **SF**
A musical about a New York man and his sophisticated girlfriend who drive to Lancaster, Pennsylvania, in order to sell a piece of property. Here they meet the Amish, a people who have held fast to their way of life in the midst of rapid change. The young couple are introduced to all aspects of the Amish way of life, including their marriage customs and the practice of shunning someone who has

broken the rules of the community. A warm comedy that takes a close look at both the New York pair and the Amish themselves.

PLAY ON!
Rick Abbot **comedy**
3m 7f **SF**

A perfect comedy for any theater group, *Play On!* is about one theater group's attempts to produce a play written by a haughty and fickle author. The first act is the disastrous rehearsal and the second is the equally horrible dress rehearsal. The final act is the opening night in which everything that can go wrong, does. At the end the author decides that she should make a speech about modern theater and sets herself up for the hilarious climax of this raucous play.

THE PLAYBOY OF THE WESTERN WORLD
J. M. Synge **drama**
7m 5f **SF**

The Playboy of the Western World is Christopher Mahon who, after arguing with his father, strikes him on the head and leaves him for dead in a ditch. He arrives at a small rural town and is immediately hailed as a hero for this dastardly deed; two of the town's women fall for him, one even jilts her tender-hearted boyfriend for the worthless playboy. In the end, Old Mahon returns and is prevented from thrashing the young man by the publican's family, who wish to have their own revenge for the trick they believe Christopher has play on them.

THE PLAYROOM
Mary Drayton **melodrama**
7m 4f **SF**

The Playroom is set in a hotel-apartment for the wealthy international jet set. Here the children of these people find themselves spoiled, jaded, and bored. To escape this life they have a Gothic hideaway in an old turret and it is in here that, spurred on by the bitter resentment of her stepmother by one of the girls, they plot to kidnap the woman's daughter and even to kill her. A truly spine-tingling thriller.

PLAYS OF AMERICA FROM AMERICAN FOLKLORE

L. E. McCullough   **collection of short plays**

variable   **S&K**

A collection of ten original plays that have been adapted from American folklore specifically for young actors. Some of the plays include: *Abe Lincoln for the Defense, The Seven Chan Brothers of Paiute Grass,* and *The Most Dangerous Woman in America.* The plays also come with optional music and easy-to-follow production information.

THE PLEDGE

Victoria Norman   **one-act tragedy**

2f   **SF**

When they were younger, two teenage girls pledged "to remain true to each other in friendship so long as we both shall live." But people grow and people change. Stacy soon finds herself with a fast, loud group—entirely unappealing to the more quiet Beth. Feeling abandoned, Beth retreats even more until the tragedy of a broken pledge becomes all to clear. An honest look into the pain of teenage suicide.

POLLYANNA

Catherine Chisholm Cushing   **comedy**

5m 6f   **SF**

Pollyanna is the beloved story of a young orphan girl who is sent to live with her maiden aunt. In spite of all of the trials that she must go through, the irrepressible Pollyanna finds something to be happy about and through this incurable optimism finds a way to share that happiness with others. First Pollyanna straightens out the romantic entanglement of her elders and then finds love for herself in the person of Jimmy. This story is about happiness and about the tender humor in all of us.

POOL'S PARADISE

Phillip King   **farce**

4m 3f   **SF**

A farce about the wacky events that take place at the vicarage of Reverend Lionel

Toop in Mertoncum-Middlewick. The story revolves around the Reverend's wife, Penelope, her maid Ida, and Ida's sweetheart, Willie Briggs. The three have entered a football pool that they believe they have won. Soon complications abound from this unexpected windfall of 20,000 pounds. A truly hilarious romp.

THE PORTRAIT THE WIND THE CHAIR

Y. York — drama

1m 2f — **Dramatic**

Takes an exuberant look at a vexing modern problem, "latchkey" children. Two sisters, home alone, create an amazing kingdom of imagination and in the process meet one of the most original theater characters ever encountered, the "Chairman"— a well-stuffed man for his sit-down part.

THE POT BOILER

Alice Gerstenberg — short play

4m 3f — **public domain**

Sud, an experienced playwright, has allowed a novice playwright, Mr. Wouldby, to watch him as he directs his actors in a melodramatic play that he has just written. The hero, the heroine, the villain and villainess, and the heroine's mother, all come on stage and listen to him control their every movement. In the surprise ending that Sud had not yet written, the young playwright suggests an ending that will be Sud's last!

PRANK

Richard Kalinoski — drama

7m 5f — **SF**

Two teenagers, Chris Lincoln and Howie DiNardo are inseparable friends who do everything together. One night, while just hanging out, they find a cardboard cutout of Frankenstein and decide to scare people with it by standing it up on the highway. Tragically, a young mother is killed along with her two-year-old son when she swerves to avoid the figure. Her sixteen-year-old daughter lives to identify the boys, and they are put on trial for manslaughter. Both families urge the boys to blame the other, but finally they admit mutual responsibility and begin the task of rebuilding their lives and their friendship.

PRECIOUS SONS

George Furth   comic drama

3m 2f   SF

A touching and humorous autobiography about the financial struggles of a
Chicago family in the 1940s. The protagonist is the youngest son who is torn
between his dream of becoming an actor and his father's wish that he finish high
school and go to college. Bea is the mother who has her own ideas about how the
family should run, and the father is faced with the decision of having to move his
family in order to gain a promotion. A real play about real emotions.

THE PREMATURE CORPSE

Mike Johnson   crime thriller

3m 3f   SF

A tangled thriller that deserves to be a surprise, *The Premature Corpse* is (decep-
tively) about Evan Jorris who has agreed to testify against the mob. His wife
Francine convinces her lover, the lawyer Larry Craig, to help her do away with her
husband. Francine is counting on the fact that her husband's government protec-
tion will believe that the mob was responsible for his death. Soon this simple plot
twists and turns until what happens and who is who becomes a host of shocking
surprises.

PRODIGY

Mary Hall Surface   drama

6m 2f   Anchorage Press

Prodigy is a moving portrayal of Mozart's early life, exploring the triumphs and
traumas of being extraordinarily gifted.

PULLMAN CAR HIAWATHA

Thorton Wilder   one-act comedy

15m 18f   SF

Thorton Wilder's remarkable play that shows a Pullman car in all possible lights.
The towns through which the car travels are personified and even the plants, the
weather, the planets, and the hours of the night have speaking parts in this

remarkable play. *Pullman Car Hiawatha* tells the poignant stories of eight passengers on the car.

PYGMALION

Bernard Shaw   **comedy**

6m 3f   **SF**

One of Shaw's finest plays, *Pygmalion* is the story of a wealthy phonetics expert who places a bet that he can take a poor flower girl with a cockney accent into a woman with a perfect accent and pass her off in high society. This play was transformed into the Academy Award–winning film, *My Fair Lady.*

Q

QUILTERS

Molly Newman & Barbara Damashek   musical

7f   **DPS**

On the surface, *Quilters* is the story of a pioneer woman and her six daughters, but more than that the play weaves a rich tapestry of scenes that reveal the terror and the beauty that was life on the frontier. The stories contain music, dancing, and drama, and it focuses on life from the point of view of women and girls. Birth, marriage, joy, illness, and death are woven together to create a "quilt" that is a breathtaking re-creation of frontier life.

R

RABBITT

David Foxton   one-act drama

15m 1f   SF

Rabbitt is an insightful play written expressly for young adults. Set in a time after the bomb, the play explores the loss of social standards and compassion in the struggle for survival and for power. The play centers on a group of teens who try to rebuild their lives in the desolation of their barren world; as they begin to repeat the mistakes of the generation before, the play explores the destruction of humanity itself.

THE RAINMAKER

N. Richard Nash   comedy

6m 1f   SF

The Rainmaker is set during a time of devastating drought in the West. Here, two brothers and their father worry about their rather plain sister growing old without marrying as much as they worry about the crops. When a charming man comes to town promising to bring rain for one hundred dollars, the family consents if only because he is so refreshing. Soon the Rainmaker turns his charms on the young girl and both rain and love come pouring down in this heart-warming comedy.

A RAISIN IN THE SUN

Lorraine Hansberry   comedy/drama

7m 3f   SF/ RH

A Raisin in the Sun is set in the 1950s and takes place in Chicago's South Side Black ghetto. The story focuses on three generations of the Younger family. Mama dreams of moving into a decent home and plans to use her deceased husband's insurance settlement to do so; the son, a chauffeur, dreams of owning his own store and being his own boss; the daughter, a liberated and ambitious young woman, wants to go to medical school. As Mama struggles to hold the family together, all of the sacrifice, trust, and love of this family is revealed. Powerful themes of Black pride, liberation, and history run throughout this play.

RAVENSCROFT

Don Nigro   **mystery**

1m 5f   **SF**

This rather dark comedy has been called the thinking person's Gothic thriller. Inspector Ruffing is in charge of investigating the death of the young manservant, Patrick. At Ravenscroft he meets five women, each dangerous and alluring in her own right: Mrs. Ravenscroft, flirtatious and chatty; her charming but possibly demented daughter; Marcy, a beautiful governess with a hidden past; Mrs. French, the cook; and Dolly, the nervous maid. Here both the Inspector and the audience are led on a labyrinth path toward truth.

THE REAL INSPECTOR HOUND

Tom Stoppard   **farce**

6m 3f   **SF**

A play within a play within a play, *The Real Inspector Hound* is marvelously funny and clever. A farce that begins with two critics, one is lustful, the other a substitute for the regular critic; the play they watch opens with a countess, her friend, and a roué; then her crippled brother arrives. They play cards and disperse but the roué is shot dead. Inspector Hound arrives, looking for the missing critic who turns out to be the roué. But this is only the beginning of this bizarre yet shrewd farce.

THE REAL QUEEN OF HEARTS AIN'T EVEN PRETTY

Brad Bailey   **comedy**

4f   **SF**

The Real Queen of Hearts Ain't Even Pretty is a wonderful opportunity for four talented young actresses. It is set in the backstage of a beauty pageant, being held in a small Alabama town in 1976. Two of the girls are competing and two are not. When the new, pretty girl wins, the action really starts in this clever and amusing comedy that has superb monologue material for the four principal actresses.

REBEL WITHOUT A CAUSE

adapt. from James Fuller   drama

13m 10f   Dramatic

Rebel Without a Cause is easily produced, requiring only a bare stage and a few representational props. The story begins with Jim who, in spite of being warned, continues to pursue Judy, the steady girlfriend of Buzz. Buzz is the leader of a gang of high school toughs and when they beat up Jim's new friend, Plato, he agrees to a test of courage. The result is both tragic and the impetus for all of these youngsters to grow up.

REGARDING ELECTRA

Maurice Valency   drama

7m 8f   DPS

Regarding Electra is an imaginative retelling of the Greek classic that juxtaposes the present-day world with the ancient past of the tragic story of Electra and her brother Orestes. The play opens in the present, a guide is giving a tour of Agamemnon's palace and as the group moves on, a young man notices a young girl and approaches her. As they speak the years fall away and soon the two young people are Electra and Orestes. When their mother and her paramour arrive, Electra is bent on revenge and the tragedy moves inexorably forward until the audience is once again faced with the ancient ruins at Mycenae.

REINDEER SOUP

Joseph Pintauro   drama

4m 5f   A. Agent

A starving family is saved by the arrival of a mysterious woman, who will rescue them from destitution by bringing them away from the barn in which they have been living. The woman herself seems somewhat supernatural, as is the appearance of the long-dead mother. All of the children are troubled in various ways.

REMEMBER ME ALWAYS

Michael Oakes & Jennifer Wells   **one-act comedy drama**

4m 5f   **SF**

Developed with teenagers in the Drama Workshop in Greenwich Village, *Remember Me Always* is an authentic account of today's urban youth. Sandy Lee, seven fellow seniors, and Slick, the crafty businessman, come together to decorate the high school gym for the Senior-So-Long Dance. As they decorate they begin to learn about each other and about themselves, vowing in the end to never forget each other and those hours spent in the old gym.

REMEMBER MY NAME

Joanna Halpert Kraus   **drama**

5m 5f   **SF**

A drama about a young girl's struggle to survive in wartime France. *Remember My Name* focuses on the young Jewish girl's flight from the Nazis and on the courageous people who help her: a priest, a nun, and a teacher who fights for the Resistance. A play based on historic accounts it is written by a popular youth author.

THE REMEMBERER

Steven Dietz   **biographical**

5m 4f 8 chorus   **ICM**

In 1964, a Native American named Joyce Simmons Cheeka began to tell her stories to educator and child drama advocate Werdna Phillips Finley. Over the next five years, Ms. Finley taped hundreds of hours of Joyce's memories of growing up as a Squaxim Indian girl in lower Puget Sound. These reminiscences were edited down to a 270-page manuscript titled *As My Sun Now Sets*. Chapter Four of the manuscript deals with Joyce being forcibly taken from her home and placed in the Tulalip Training School, a government-run boarding school under the jurisdiction of the Bureau of Indian Affairs. That is where the play begins.

RIMERS OF ELDRITCH

Lanford Wilson   **drama**
7m 10f   **DPS**

Lanford Wilson's play about a murder in a small middle-western town. The play looks straight into the hearts of its characters: a middle-age woman in love with the young man working in her cafe; a coarse and unpleasant woman who mistreats her senile mother; and the relationship between a young man and a crippled young woman. Exploring the very fabric of Bible Belt America, Wilson creates a vivid and unflinching portrait of the town called Eldritch.

THE RISE AND RISE OF DANIEL ROCKET

Peter Parnell   **play**
5m 5f   **DPS**

Daniel Rocket is a young man who is convinced that he can fly; as a twelve-year-old boy he is ridiculed and shunned by his peers, even by the young girl he adores. Forced into proving himself, Daniel really does fly and soon becomes wealthy and famous. He returns to his home town twenty years later, a symbol of genius but still isolated from those around him. As their continued distrust creates a growing uncertainty, Daniel's gift wanes. One last, fatal flight ends the life of this remarkable man and his unique gift.

THE RIVALS

R. V. Sheridan   **comedy**
9m 4f   **public domain**

The Rivals is Richard Brinsley Sheriden's splendidly witty drawing room comedy that first gave the theatrical world such wonderful characters as Mrs. Malaprop.

THE ROARING TWENTIES

Edward Trigger   **comedy**
6m 8f   **SF**

The Roaring Twenties is a nostalgic journey back to the fads and foibles of this remarkable time in American history. It centers around the Denning family: Dexter, the temperamental husband; Jessie, the practical mother; and their three children. Soon this average family is disrupted by the arrival of Jessie's rebellious brother who decides to stay with them. A month later, with the brother still there, someone opens an account with Jessie's name and deposits ten thousand dollars. A humorous look at the Roaring Twenties.

ROCK A BYE DADDY

John O'Donnell   comedy

3m 4f   SF

An indulgent look at American middle-class life, youth, and the women's liberation movement. The Considine family seems normal enough, that is until the mother leaves for a national campaign for Women's Lib; the daughter, Peggy, moves out of the house for reasons that she won't entirely reveal; and young Louie gets picked up by the police. Mr. Considine tries to keep it all together, finally deciding that laughter rules the days.

ROMEO AND JULIET

William Shakespeare   tragedy

17m 4f   public domain

Feuding families cannot stop Romeo and Juliet from falling in love, but they can stop them from living happily ever after. One of the saddest of Shakespeare's tragedies, the young lovers kill themselves, each believing the other to be already dead. A lively cast of supporting actors provide lighter moments, making the end all the more heartrending.

A ROOMFUL OF ROSES

Edith Sommer   comedy/drama

4m 5f   DPS

A Roomful of Roses is the story of Bridget, a young girl who had been abandoned by her mother and reared by her bitter father. Now that her father is ready to remarry, he sends Bridget to her mother, where she meets her mother, her stepfather, and two friendly neighborhood children. Although Bridget is aloof, defensive, and scared to love, her new family and friends manage to get through to her. When she finds out the truth behind why her father sent her to her mother, it threatens to undo all of the trust Bridget has taught herself to feel, but the sincere love of her mother and friends wins the day.

RUNAWAYS

Elizabeth Swados   **musical**

11m 9f   **SF**

Runaways is a unique collection of songs performed by runaway children of all different ages. Although the play is primarily about the lives, hopes, dreams, and sorrows of runaway children from broken homes, this touching musical takes the audience as well as the actors beyond that subject and comments on the world in which these children live.

S

SAINT JOAN

Bernard Shaw   **drama**

22m 3f   **SF**

Considered by many to be Shaw's masterpiece, *Saint Joan* follows the life of Joan of Arc from the moment when she appears to her regional governor to the moment when she meets the Dauphin, to the siege of Orleans, the coronation at Rheims, and finally to her trial and death at the stake. Throughout the play run the themes of nationalism and the rise of Protestantism.

SAME TIME NEXT YEAR

Bernard Slade   **comedy**

1m 1f   **SF**

A wonderful look at the changes time has wrought in American culture. *Same Time Next Year* revolves around a man and a woman who are perfectly happy with their lives but who meet once a year to continue their adulterous affair. George starts out as a stuffy workaholic and evolves into a born-again hippie while Doris begins as an awkward young woman, becomes a restless housewife, an over-age flower child, and finally a career woman. The six scenes, five years apart, are interposed with news clips, speeches, and sports news of the time.

SCENES AND REVELATIONS

Elan Garonzik   **drama**

3m 4f   **SF**

In 1894, during the height of America's westward expansion, four sisters from Pennsylvania decide to leave their farm and birthplace forever, but to go to England not to the great frontier. As they prepare for their journey, a series of lyrical flashbacks documents each of the sisters' frustrations in love until the final scene leaves the four sisters united in their quest for a better life in England.

SCHOOL FOR WIVES

Molière   comedy

8m 3f   public domain

School for Wives is Molière's play about a fifty-year-old man, Arnolphe, who, although rich, has delayed marriage for fear of being cuckolded. He finally decides to marry the innocent young Agnes, who he has educated in convents, away from the world. Her innocence is her undoing as she does not expect baser motives from the men she meets. Finally, Agnes meets Horace and they fall in love; not knowing that she is engaged to Arnolphe, Horace confesses his love to her. Finally, Agnes's father returns and announces that he will marry her to a friend of the family, Horace.

SCOOTER THOMAS...

Peter Parnell   drama

2m   DPS

The play opens with Dennis, who has just received a phone call from his mother telling him that his best friend during his boyhood years has died. As he packs to attend the funeral, Dennis begins to recall those years with Scooter: the pranks, their first loves, the separation during the college years. While all his friends went on to pursue careers and marriages, Scooter stayed behind, working in the Post Office until he became convinced that there was nothing to live for. The play is comprised of a series of scenes between Dennis, Scooter, and other characters also played by Dennis.

THE SEAGULL

Anton Chekhov   drama

7m 6f   DPS

Chekhov's classic play of the modern theater, *The Seagull* is set on the estate of the wealthy Sorin and weaves the lives of the characters, including the beautiful actress Madame Arkadina, her sensitive son, and Trigorin—the charming and successful writer. All the hopes, dreams, loves, and disappointments of their lives come together in this compelling tapestry of the human experience.

SECOND CLASS
Brad Slaight   **drama**
3m 5f   **Baker's**
Scott is a cyberspace Cyrano, Maggie and Herm communicate only through pre-recorded tapes played on boom-boxes, and Andrew is tormented by his peers because of his scars. These, and other teens, are part of a troupe of students experiencing the travails of out-of-class encounters in high school. Adding to the tapestry of his successful *Class Action,* Slaight digs further into the extraordinary world of today's youth.

THE SECRET GARDEN
Marsha Norman & Lucy Simon   **musical**
11m 10f   **SF**
The enchanting children's favorite in the form of a dazzling musical, this version of *The Secret Garden* contains flashback scenes, dream sequences, a chorus of ghosts, and an unforgettable musical score. It is the story of an eleven-year-old orphaned girl who is sent to live with her reclusive uncle and a crippled boy in a Yorkshire estate. This is a compelling tale of regeneration and the power of love.

THE SECRET HISTORY OF THE FUTURE
James Still   **one-act comedy drama**
5m 3f   **SF**
The Secret History of the Future takes a humorous leap into the past with three teenagers who have travelled back into time and find themselves in fifteenth- century Spain. Here they meet Diego Columbus, the heir to the throne, Mona Lisa, and an eccentric man named Leonardo da Vinci. They run up against the Inquisition and the prejudices of the time. The remarkable aspect of this play is its ability to offer a more in-depth look at the history too often fed to children in two-dimensional textbooks. Well-received by both middle school and high school audiences.

THE SECRET LIFE OF WALTER MITTY

Joe Manchester, Leon Carr, & Earl Shuman   musical

5m 6f   SF

A musical comedy based on the book by James Thurber. *The Secret Life of Walter Mitty* is about Walter Mitty's reflections on his rather boring life. Taking place on his fortieth birthday, we see the secret life that Walter has created for himself, a series of stories in which he is always the hero. These stories become so real to him that the line between fantasy and reality is comically blurred. In spite of Willa de Wisp's attempts to lure him from his family into the secret life, in the end Walter finds himself happily fixed in the real world.

A SEPARATE PEACE

Nancy Pahl Gilsenan adapt. from Knowles   drama

8m   Dramatic

Adapted from the book by John Knowles, *A Separate Peace* is the story of two boys who stand on the threshold of manhood in a country on the brink of war. The first is Gene Forrester, a careful, studious boy who fears what the future may bring. At a New England summer school, he meets Phineas whose love of life defies the grim reality of drafts and ignorant authority. The two become fast friends until the fear in Gene overcomes the life in Finny. A tragic look into the anxious era of 1942.

THE SEVEN CHAN BROTHERS OF PAIUTE PASS

L.E. McCullough   one-act

17m 5f   S&K

A play with a parallel structure shifting between the present and late nineteenth-century America. In the 1890s setting, seven brothers battled the oppressive prejudice of anti-foreigner discrimination. The story concentrates on the enduring belief in one's inner strength and confidence in following the path of good.

SHAKIN' THE MESS OUTTA MISERY

Shay Youngblood   drama

8w   Dramatic

Simply the story of a young Black girl coming of age in the South during the 1960s, *Shakin' the Mess Outta Misery* focuses on Daughter, the twenty-five-year-old narrator who recounts how her many Big Mamas helped raise her in a non-traditional way. As Daughter remembers her childhood, the women enter to tell their own remarkable stories. A heartfelt story of the tightknit community of African-American women making their way during a turbulent time.

THE SHAYNA MAIDEL

Barbara Lebow   drama

2m 4f   DPS

A powerful and haunting look at the aftermath of the Holocaust as seen through the eyes of one family. *The Shayna Maidel* revolves around the Weiss family. Rose is the Americanized daughter of Mordecai who fled his native Poland to start a new life in America. His other daughter and wife were never able to follow them due to the arrival of the Nazis. Finally, the eldest daughter manages to be reunited with her family. Old World clashes with New until Rose realizes, with the help of a letter sent to her by her dead mother, that this is a time for new hope and joy in the family.

SHE STOOPS TO CONQUER: OR, THE MISTAKES OF NIGHT

Robert M. Singleton   one-act comedy

7m 4f   Dramatic

An adaptation of a longer British comedy that brings to life all of the humor and wit of the original, *She Stoops to Conquer* is the story of Mr. Hastings who goes to the country to meet his bride-to-be. There he and his friend mistake the house of his bride for the country inn. The young woman discovers the mistake and uses it to force the young man to court her without the pretensions of society. A colorful play about the complexities of Georgian England with memorably funny characters.

SHE WAS LOST, AND IS FOUND
Richard Hensley   **one-act drama**
1m 2f   **SF**
She Was Lost, and Is Found opens with Ellen and Dan Clark anxiously awaiting the return of their runaway teenage daughter, Janie. The couple search through their past in an attempt to explain Janie's unhappiness but can find no simple answers. Their anxiety increases when Sue, the older and always obedient daughter, displays unease and even resentment at the return of Janie. Eventually all three, Ellen, Dan, and Sue find truths about themselves that will help to reunite their broken family.

SHERLOCK HOLMES AND THE CURSE OF THE SIGN OF FOUR
Dennis Rosa   **Victorian melodrama**
6-9m 1f   **DPS**
The classic Sherlock tale in which Holmes and Watson for the first time battle the evil Dr. Moriarty. At stake in this tale of stolen treasure and murder is the life of the lovely Mary Morstan, whose late father left for her the riches of a long-lost treasure. The ensuing quest to find the riches leads to danger for Holmes, romance for Watson, and high adventure for all. Thrills and laughter combine in this romantic adventure of one of the world's most beloved crime fighters.

SHERLOCK'S LAST CASE
Charles Marowitz   **thriller**
5m 2f   **DPS**
A dazzling thriller with twists and turns that develop well-known characters in a new light. *Sherlock's Last Case* pits Holmes against the son of the diabolic Moriarty who desires revenge for the doctor's death. Holmes eventually finds himself in love with Moriarty's daughter and trapped by the bitterly resentful Watson. A thriller with a shocking end, little suspected but eagerly awaited.

SHIVAREE

William Mastrosimone   **drama**

1m 2f   **SF**

William Mastrosimone's play about a young hemophiliac who has been kept sheltered by his cab-driver mother, by necessity. Chandler is intelligent but naive and longs for contact with the outside world. His chance for love finally comes in the form of Shivaree, a neighbor who makes a living as an itinerant belly dancer. Soon the young people fall in love, much to the dismay of Chandler's mother who forbids her son to see Shivaree again. Chandler's moment of triumph comes when he finally has the courage to climb out of his sheltered home and pursue his true love.

SHOOTING STARS

Molly Newman   **comdy**

1m 7f   **DPS**

Set during Christmas week in 1962, the place is a locker room in a small, run-down gymnasium. Here a touring women's basketball team, the Shooting Stars, prepares to face-off against the local men's team. The high-spirited and mostly Southern girls reveal their own distinct personalities and inner selves. When their domineering and paternalistic coach, Cassius, falls dead from a heart attack the young women must, for the first time, decide their own fate. The result of which is a dazzling and triumphant ending to this fast-moving comedy.

SHREW!

Richard A. Barbie   **musical**

6m 6f variable chrorus   **Dramatic**

A musical adaptation of William Shakespeare's *The Taming of the Shrew.* Written to be fast paced and full of fun, *Shrew* maintains all of the wit and flavor of the original while rendering this contemporary version in more comprehensible terms. Wonderful music and a constant barrage of punchlines and sight gags will have audiences standing in the aisles.

SIGHTINGS
Brad Slaight   one-act comedy
2m 1f   Baker's

Two childhood friends come together on Prom night. One has left her date at the bottom of the mountain on which the other is sitting waiting for the aliens to come and take him away. When Julie's date arrives and begins to make fun of Jarred, we see childhood loyalty in conflict with the more complicated issues of adolescence and insecurity.

SIX CHARACTERS IN SEARCH OF AN AUTHOR
Luigi Pirandello   drama
12m 8f   SF

A group of actors prepare to rehearse their play until they are interrupted by another troupe who are searching for an author for their tragedy. As the two groups come together to act out the story that is the strangers' lives, the "real" performers get a lesson in acting and in life. A play about the theater, about belief, and about the very nature of truth.

THE SKIN OF OUR TEETH
Thornton Wilder   fantasy
5m 5f   SF

Thorton Wilder's satiric fantasy about the incredible lives of the Antrobus family. *The Skin of Our Teeth* traces the family history from the time of war, any war, and through the struggle to survive flood, pestilence, fire, and dozens of wars. Having survived a thousand disasters "by the skin of their teeth," the Antrobuses reveal what heroes are truly made of, equal parts courage and foolishness, and finally what faith in humanity can accomplish.

THE SLAB BOYS
John Byrne   comedy
6m 2f   SF

The Slab Boys of Byrne's comedy are Scottish teenage boys from the working class; they work in factories and are victims of their culture's rigid class struggle and economic status. Trying to hold on to their dreams, the Slab Boys battle their bosses, complacency, and their own frustration to try to make it out of their confining world. The focus of this insightful comedy is whether or not Phil, the smartest of the boys, can get accepted into a school.

SMOKE AND MIRRORS
Osborne & Anthony Will Herrera   **mystery**
4m 1f   **SF**
With a simple set and only five characters, this mystery-comedy keeps audiences guessing until the final scene. *Smoke and Mirrors* is set on an isolated, island estate in Mississippi. A producer-director and his screenwriter plot to rid themselves of the insufferable star using a botched rehearsal of a suicide scene. Soon the bumbling local sheriff is on the scene, digging up one surprise after another.

SNAP JUDGEMENTS
Walden Theater   **comedy/drama**
variable   **Dramatic**
Written by talented young playwrights, this evening of theater is a series of short pieces juxtaposed with the interaction of a girl and a boy. The work opens with the boy unwrapping a Snickers bar; as the girl watches him, she explains why a relationship with this person would be unthinkable. Their story becomes more and more complex as the audience is returned to this drama within a drama.

SNOW LEOPARDS
Martin Jones   **comic drama**
2f   **SF**
A haunting comedy set in Chicago. *Snow Leopards* takes place in the Lincoln Park Zoo, in front of the snow leopards' cage. It tells the story of two sisters who have left their home in West Virginia. Sally has recently run away to find her older sister Claire June who she imagines to have been living a life wholly unlike her trapped existence in their hometown. Although the two girls both discover that life in the North is not everything they thought it would be, they agree to stay and make a new life. This play is simple to produce with a wealth of scene and monologue material.

SOMETIMES I WAKE UP IN THE MIDDLE OF THE NIGHT

Walden Theat. Conserv. Play Writing Program NY   comedy/drama

10-20   **Dramatic**

A profound look into the expression of our inner most hopes and fears that often strike us in the middle of the night. Written by the talented playwrights from the Walden Theatre Conservatory, this play is a series of scenes and monologues that comprise a full evening of absorbing theater. The pieces range from funny, sad, to disturbing, but they are always real, exploring the sometimes painful and sometimes exuberant experiences of today's youth.

SORRY

Timothy Mason   **one-act**

1m 1f   **ICM**

Set in a small one-room apartment in New York's East Village, this one-act play revolves around the interaction of two good-looking twentysomethings, Pat and Wayne. Pat has accidently shot Wayne as a result of her violent experiences in New York and the rest of the play examines what this introduction says about who these two young people are and what they are looking for.

THE SOUND OF MUSIC

Rodgers & Hammerstein   **musical**

9m 15f   **RHML**

Set in Austria during World War II and Hitler's reign of terror, *The Sound of Music* is based on the true story of the Von Trapp Family and the woman who changed their lives. Maria comes to the Von Trapp home as a nanny to the children but eventually wins a permanent place in their hearts. This heart-warming, epic adventure is accompanied by memorable songs and unforgettable characters.

SOUTHERN CROSS

Jon Klein   **drama**

8-17m 3-4f   **DPS**

A panoramic look into southern American history, *Southern Cross* is an epic-style play that looks to the past in order to explain the present. Familiar stories and historical figures interact here, sharing the stage with lesser-known people and events that together resonate with the power of a remarkable history. Characters include Sherman, Martin Luther King, Elvis, a fugitive slave, and a steamboat captain among others. The chilling climax arrives with the interaction of all of these stories.

THE SPELLING BEE

Marsha Sheiness   black comedy

4m 4f   SF

A black comedy about four children—characters written to be played by older actors—who compete for the honor of being crowned the nation's best speller. The suspense of this taut comedy holds throughout as each of the children's mothers is determined that her child shall be the victor and as the Quizzer preps them for a leap into the "Big Time."

THE SPIRAL STAIRCASE

F. Andrew Leslie   mystery/drama

4m 4f   DPS

Adapted from one of Hollywood's most popular thrillers, *The Spiral Staircase* is a drama-mystery that opens with the village constable arriving at the Warren house to report yet another unexplained murder. All of the victims have been young girls with some noticeable defect including young Helen, unable to speak since witnessing her parents' death. Neither Mrs. Warren not anyone else has seen Helen since the morning and when she arrives, all of her protectors begin to abandon her. The suspense and horror of this work will have audiences on the edge of their seats.

THE SPIRIT OF CHRISTMAS

Tom Fuller   Christmas drama

5, 13-52 extras   Dramatic

A unique adaptation of Dickens's classic tale. Whatever happened to the reformed Ebenezer after his haunting Christmas Eve? He married and had a son, who also had a son who moved to America. The grandson of Ebenezer had a daughter, Ernestina, who is the leading lady of this play. A play especially suited for high school groups, *The Spirit of Christmas* has many wonderful roles for women actors.

THE SPLENDID VOYAGE OF KITTY DOYLE

L.E. McCullough   one-act

8m 10f   S&K

This is a play based on the historical incident of a ship, *The Atlantic,* full of immigrants that foundered off the coast of Newfoundland in 1873. The story is told in parallel segments—a present-day trip in a jetliner, and the ocean-crossing voyage of the steamship—focusing on the experiences of a young girl, Jennifer, and her great-great-grandmother, Kitty Doyle. It is a play of high adventure, heartfelt emotion, and inspiration.

SPLENDOR IN THE GRASS

F. Andrew Lelsie from Inge   drama

4m 5f   DPS

Splendor in the Grass is an honest and touching look at teenage love. It is the story of Bud Stamper, a star athlete and son of the richest man in town. Deanie is the girl lucky enough to catch him. The two young people soon find themselves forced to confront the powerful feelings between them, but they are thwarted by Bud's father who pushes him toward Yale in preparation for taking over the family oil business. Bud pushes Deanie away until she winds up in an institution because she is emotionally unstable. After she is released she learns that the Depression has wiped out the Stamper fortune. Bud has married a New Haven waitress and Deanie is engaged to a man she met in the hospital. The final touching scene where the two reconcile the past with the new present is truly touching.

SPOILS OF WAR

Michael Weller   drama

3m 3f   SF

Well-known comic author Michael Weller follows the desperate attempts of a young boy trying to reconcile his divorced parents. The Fifties are explored in this play through the eyes of Martin's parents: His mother, Elyse, still wants to live for something, for a cause; and his father Andrew, a disillusioned activist has slipped back into the system. Caught between two opposite life views, Martin is finally faced with the direction his own life will take.

SPOON RIVER ANTHOLOGY
Charles Aidman adapted from Edgar Lee Masters   monologues
3m 2f   **SF**
Adapted from Edgar Lee Master's collection of vignettes, this play introduces the audience to some sixty characters who are now inhabitants of the town cemetery and who have brought with them to the grave their life secrets. Humorous, touching, and sometimes bitter, these characters range from young lovers to preachers, teachers, and even include a Jewish man who wound up in the wrong cemetery. A wonderfully diverse and constantly entertaining collection.

SPRING'S AWAKENING
Frank Wedekind, trans. Eric Bentley   drama
31m 6f   **SF**
Frank Wedekind's brilliant play about the tragedy of awakening sexuality in an atmosphere of repression and denial. This play explores the possibility that parents and teachers are responsible for the tragedy of youth because of their attitudes toward sex.

STAGE DOOR
Edna Ferber & George F. Kaufman   comedy
11m 21f   **DPS**
Stage Door revolves around a group of young girls who have come to New York to study acting and find jobs to support themselves. The sixteen young women live in Mrs. Orcutt's boardinghouse, and their lives are presented in a series of scenes both comedic and tragic as some of the girls give up their dreams. The central figure is the talented and tenacious Terry Randall who, with the help of her friend David, manages to persevere.

STAND-UP TRAGEDY
Bill Cain   drama
9m   **SF**
Tom Griffin teaches at a Catholic school in New York's Lower East Side. His students are primarily Hispanic boys, and Mr. Griffin attempts to save one of them

in particular, a talented artist named Lee Cortez. Lee's violent home life is presented. The actor who plays Lee will also play his slatternly mother and his jealous brother. Eventually the brother, unable to bear Lee's success, murders him. A student's-eye view of the world is offered in this play that also has rap numbers interspersed.

STARMITES
Barry Keating & Stuart Ross   **musical**
6m 6f   **SF**
A galactic musical about a young girl who dreams her way into a comic book adventure and eventually saves the galaxy. Eleanor and her friends—the Starmites, Spacepunk, and the lizard man—must fight the powerful forces of evil. Replete with space-age humor and science fiction references, this zany musical offers a lighthearted look into the world of the comic book, and beyond.

STATE OF REVOLUTION
Robert Bolt   **play**
20m 5f   **SF**
Chronicling the period from 1910–1920, *State of Revolution* traces the historical events of the Russian Revolution in the early twentieth century. The play brings to life the key characters involved in the Revolution, following the life of Lenin from 1910 in Gorky's villa on Capri to right after his death when his recommendation to dismiss Stalin is suppressed and ignored. A thoughtful and accessible history play.

STEEL MAGNOLIAS
Robert Harling   **plays**
6f   **DPS**
Steel Magnolias is set in a beauty parlor in Chinquapin, Louisianna. Truvy is the outspoken owner of the parlor where anyone who is anyone gets her hair done; Truvy is assisted by Annelle, who remains uncertain as to whether she is in fact still married. Other characters are the town's rich old grump, Ouiser, an eccentric millionaire; the town's social queen and her daughter Shelby, a beautiful young

girl about to be married. Together these women experience humor and tragedy, learning about themselves and drawing on the strength of their friendship.

STEPHEN VINCENT BENÉT'S STORIES OF AMERICA
Stephen Vincent Benét   **narrative theater**
min. 3m 3f, flexible   **DPS**

This unique blending of story, poetry, and music draws on the fanciful tales of Stephen Vincent Benét. This creative evening of theater focuses mainly on the Colonial years, through the Revolution and the western expansion. The American Experience is truly brought to life with drama, song, and poetry, creating a kaleidoscope of wisdom that brings to life the American past while offering a look into contemporary society.

STONEWATER RAPTURE
Doug Wright   **short play**
1m 1f   **DPS**

Set in a small Texas town, *Stonewater Rapture* is the story of Carlyle and Whitney, two eighteen-year-olds. Carlyle is devoted to her religion and is saving herself for God. Whitney is her best friend, but he has had trouble at school because the other guys think he is gay. When he tries to get Carlyle to sleep with him, she refuses and tells him her divine destiny; he leaves, angry and hurt. Three weeks later he returns to her house only to find out that she has been gang-raped by the football team and has convinced herself that it was God's will. She is pregnant and wants him to marry her. Somehow the misunderstood pair manage to find each other in this violent world.

STREET SCENE
Elmer Rice   **drama**
16m 11f   **SF**

The rumbling of passing trains and the shrill piercing of their whistles accompanies this look into the comedy and tragedy of daily life. *Street Scenes* is a slice of life taken from a poor neighborhood. At the center of this remarkable play is a man whose wife is having a sordid affair with the milkman; upon the husband's return, he kills them both, crystallizing a moment and also an entire neighborhood in one dramatic scene.

SUICIDE IN B-FLAT

Sam Shepard   **mysterious overture**

3m 2f   **SF**

In Sam Shepard's bizarre comedy, two young private eyes try to uncover the mystery behind a famous jazz musician, Niles. As they stumble through Shepard's notorious metaphysical world, the two men try to discover not only who the culprit is but also who is the victim! An original play and one of Shepard's finest.

T

TAKE A GIANT STEP
Louis Peterson   **drama**
7m 7f   **SF**

Take a Giant Step chronicles the coming of age of a Black boy; it is the story of the bewildering confrontation with an almost indecipherable adult world. Sensing a growing estrangement from his white friends and having been expelled from school, the young boy goes to a saloon where he is propositioned by a harlot. He flees for home only to have his parents scold him. When he becomes ill, a long talk with the family maid gives him insight that finally allows him to grow.

A TALE OF TWO CITIES
adapt. Fitzgibbons   **drama**
16m 10f   **SF**

An adaptation of Dickens's novel about the horrors of the French Revolution. An ingenious setting solves the problem of the novels many locations and four narrators, each an innkeeper, bring the action of this stunning novel to life. Nothing is left behind: the riots, the trials, and the guillotine, Lucie and Jarvis Lorry, Sydney Carton, and the DeFarges.

TALKING BONES
Shay Youngblood   **drama**
2m 3f   **Dramatic**

Shay Youngblood's play about three women who hear voices and how they reconcile those voices with the cynical world around them. Ruth is a dignified bohemian trying to settle her affairs before she dies; Ruth has always heard the voices and interprets them to have special meaning in her life. Her daughter, BayBay, is a rather gaudy woman, slightly out of step and looking for a way to escape the trapped life of caring for her mother. She too hears the voices but often ignores or misinterprets them. Eila, BayBay's child, plays the role of bridge-maker between these two views. At the end of this complex but rewarding journey, the joyous whispers of the ancestors bring hope to all.

TALKING PICTURES

Horton Foote   drama

6m 5f   DPS

Pulitzer Prize–winning author Horton Foote has set this play in the small town of Harrison, Texas, in 1929. The play revolves around Myra Tolliver and her struggle to support herself and her son, Peter. Other characters include the Jacksons who own the boardinghouse where Myra lives and teaches piano to their two daughters; Willy, the bricklayer in love with Myra; Peter's father, Gerard; and Willie's ex-wife. A full drama of a young woman's attempt to create a life for herself in a changing world.

TALLEY & SON

Lanford Wilson   drama

6m 6f   DPS

The third play in Wilson's series about the Talley family in Lebanon, Missouri. *Talley & Son* takes place on Independence Day in 1944 with the horror of WWII pervading the play. The elder Mr. Talley is senile, his life illuminated by bursts of almost violent lucidity where he sees the empire he helped build fall to pieces in the hands of the younger, incompetent generation. The petty scandals and selfishness of the family are commented on by the ghost of the second son, Timmy, who, unbeknownst to his family, has died in the Pacific war.

TARTUFFE

Molière   comedy

8m 4f   SF

Considered by some to be Molière's best farce, *Tartuffe* is the story of Orgon, a naive man who turns over his house, fortune, even his daughter to the title character who is nothing more than a swindling hypocrite with religious pretensions. After banishing his son for suggesting that Tartuffe and Orgon's wife are having an affair, Orgon's wife manages to convince him of Tartuffe's duplicity. Only intervention by the royal courts, however, prevents Tartuffe from leaving Orgon and his family penniless.

TARTUFFE

adapt. by Noyce Burleson   one-act farce
5m 5f   Dramatic

A prize-winning one-act version of Molière's classic farce. Perfect for talented high school students, this play begins with a prologue in which Molière must deal with his acting company that leads into the play itself.

TEACH ME HOW TO CRY

Patricia Joudry   play
3m 7f   DPS

A delicately written play about two youngsters who manage to find each other and an identity in a world to which they feel little connection. The young girl, proud and self-conscious, guesses that her mother was never actually married; the young boy considers himself "the writing type," but his ambitious parents try to push him toward what they consider to be better things. Outcasts in the high school world of gossip, they slowly find each other and a bit of happiness.

THE TEAHOUSE OF THE AUGUST MOON

John Patrick   comedy
18m 8f, 3children 1goat   DPS

An acclaimed comedy based on the novel by Vern Sneider, *The Teahouse of the August Moon* follows the career of an Army Occupation officer stationed in Okinawa. He is assigned to teach democracy to the natives and in spite of the rigid Colonel watching his every move, he falls for the charms of the local residents. Finding himself the owner of a Geisha girl and his schoolhouse materials being used to build a teahouse, the young officer even resorts to selling the local brandy to stationed officers. As the teahouse is unveiled, the Colonel makes an unwelcome appearance and only Congress can save the day.

TEARS OF MY SISTER

Horton Foote   one-act drama
3m 4f   DPS

One of four short plays in Horton Foote's collection about love, longing, and redemption. *Tears of My Sister* is about a young woman who watches her sister try, and ultimately fail, to avoid marrying a man whom she does not love. Both Cecilia and Bessie learn the hard lesson that life is not always fair as they come of age in their own touching way.

TEECHERS
John Godber   comedy
2m 1f   SF

Three actors play twenty-one roles in this very flexible, fast-paced comedy. *Teechers* invokes life in a modern public high school through the lens of three student actors who show the progress of the much-criticized and misunderstood drama teacher. The comedy runs the gamut of emotions. When the teacher finally leaves the school for a private one, the teenagers' despair offers a sobering counterpoint to the humor of the play.

TELL ME ANOTHER STORY, SING ME A SONG
Jean Lenox Toddie   one-act
2f   SF

A lighthearted look at the relationship between a mother and her daughter. *Tell Me Another Story, Sing Me Another Song* is a two-character play about the conflicts that can arise between a mother and her daughter—and at the love that can resolve those conflicts. The play's themes include the emotions that come with a daughter's emergence from childhood to adolescence and with how both mothers and daughters deal with adulthood and aging.

TELL ME THAT YOU LOVE ME, JUNIE MOON
D. D. Brooke from Kellogg   drama
6m 6f   Dramatic

A play that is both comic and tragic, simultaneously happy and sad. *Tell Me That You Love Me, Junie Moon* is the story of three resilient young people who have each been tragically handicapped. Junie Moon, Arthur, and Warren meet in a hospital and band together, drawn by their common humor and strength, and leaning on each other for support. The three friends soon find that together they can face the world and lead fulfilling lives.

TEN LITTLE INDIANS
Agatha Christie   **mystery**
8m 3f   **SF**
A perfect mystery selection, Agatha Christie's *Ten Little Indians* is a mystery, comedy, and suspenseful fantasy. The plot revolves around ten little indians lined up on a mantlepiece of a country house. Each indian comes with a rhyme explaining his death. Eight guests, strangers to each other, are mysteriously invited to the house and they, along with the two servants, soon find themselves trapped in a deadly and mysterious parallel to the ten little Indians.

THE TENTH MAN
Paddy Chayefsky   **comedy**
12m 1f   **SF**
A comedy set in an old meeting room that is now used as a Jewish temple. Here a rabbi and various Jews meet for prayer on a wintry Saturday. Not all of the men, however, are devout: One is a young atheist who jokes that he comes to temple merely to keep warm and another is a agnostic lawyer, desperately unhappy and kept from suicide by barely effectual therapy. Another character is that of an older man who has brought his granddaughter to the temple because he believes she is possessed by a dybbuk. As the girl drifts from lucidity to insanity, an exorcism is prepared—with surprising results.

TEVYA AND HIS DAUGHTERS
Arnold Perl   **play**
6m 6f   **DPS**
A wonderful play based on the stories by Sholom Alaeichem. *Tevya and His Daughters* is an adaptation of those stories into a one delightful play. The main action of the play centers around Tevya and his wife's attempts to marry off their two oldest daughters. The first, Tzeitl, has attracted the attention of a wealthy butcher but instead falls for the poor tailor. When love wins, Tevya and Golde focus their hopes on Hodel. Unfortunately, Hodel is already in love with a poor student and when he is exiled to Siberia, she chooses to follow him there. The play ends with Tevya contemplating the futures of his other five daughters.

THERE'S A BOY IN THE GIRLS' BATHROOM

Louis Sachar   comedy/drama

5m 8f   SSA

This story takes place in contemporary America. The kids are in the fifth grade. Carla, a school counselor, is young and pretty. She dresses in funky, hip clothes. She makes great strides in helping Bradley (a very insecure boy) deal with his fears and make new friends. Unfortunately, the parents of the students cause the school to fire this new faculty member. She's considered a threat. We see Carla develop and nurture relationships with the students, and we see them grow up and grow closer in her short tenure there. This play is emotionally draining with a very happy ending.

THIN AIR: TALES FROM A REVOLUTION

Lynne Alvarez   drama

10m 5f   JKA

Lynne Alvarez's *Thin Air: Tales from a Revolution* is a boldly theatrical play set against the tumultuous backdrop of a fictitious South American country in the midst of a revolution. The story concerns Anya, the daughter of American Alexander Young and Hilda Inez Santa Maria de Young, a well-born South American. Anya's family came to this part of the world to focus on Alexander's research of cultural music. During their time in the provinces, Alexander's secret political involvement separates him from the family. While searching for her father, Anya is abducted at the gates of the local prison, never to be reunited with her parents. Through the course of the play, which moves back and forth in time, we see Anya's parents in the United States trying to piece together their daughter's abduction and Anya in prison, grappling for answers about her father and clinging to life.

THE THIRD DAUGHTER

Mario Fratti   drama

3m 4f   SF

The Third Daughter is Mario Fratti's drama about a wealthy Italian father who has three daughters. Although he is very strict with the first two, he mysteriously allows the youngest daughter many freedoms, including allowing her to meet a young man in his own apartment. Why does he allow this? We find that this daughter is the offspring of his wife's adulterous affair and he has conceived a scheme whereby he will destroy both women.

THIS IS A TEST

Stephen Gregg   **one-act comedy**

13-15, flexible   **Dramatic**

A ticking clock counts down the sixty allotted minutes for this test that is supposed to predict your future. The teacher doesn't like you, you never saw the review sheet, your classmates are cheating, and the final essay question is in Chinese. To make matters worse, there are voices in your head that just won't stop reminding you that no matter how badly this test is going, your personal life is worse. A comedy about every student's worse nightmare.

THE THREE MUSKETEERS

Peter Raby   **drama**

20m 5f   **DPS**

A wonderful adaptation of Alexander Dumas's beloved story. *The Three Musketeers* chronicles the adventures of D'Artagnan and his fellow musketeers, Athos, Porthos, and Aramis. The four men fight for country and king, reveling in wine, women, and song on the way. Other well-known characters, including the evil Cardinal Richelieu and the beautiful Constance Bonacieux, are here as well as the memorable plots, counterplots, and triumphs of good over evil that have made this adventure story a classic.

THREE WAYS HOME

Casey Kurtti   **drama**

1m 2f   **SF**

Three Ways Home is a drama composed of monologues by three characters: a Black woman, her disturbed son, and the social worker sent to help the boy. Dawn is a wizened mother with four kids; her first three are fine, but Frankie seems to have fallen into an invented world populated by super-hero friends. The social worker, truly committed to helping the family, meets resistance from Dawn at first, but eventually they unite for the common goal of saving Frankie.

THE THRONE OF OSIRIS
L.E. McCullough   one-act
7m 7f   S&K
The religion of the ancient Egyptians is rich with many tales of their very large pantheon of more than fifty major deities. This play teaches us about Osiris, the Egyptian god of the Underworld, and the eternal conflict between the gods, Seth (Osiris's brother) and Horus (Osiris's son), who are always seeking his approval.

THURBER CARNIVAL
James Thurber   musical
4m 4f   SF
A musical revue created by one of America's leading humorists and perfect for all groups, even those without any drop of musical talent! A series of sketches of American life at its funniest, interposed with music. Sketches include a fable about the unicorn in the garden, a tale of Gentle Shoppers who rely on martinis to get them through a spree, scenes from *The Secret Life of Sir Walter Mitty*, and even stories about Thurber himself.

A TIDE OF VOICES
Suzanne Granfield   drama
4m 1f   SF
Set during the time of the American Revolution, this play is a series of vignettes that focuses on the effects on ordinary people of this turbulent time. Stories include one about a man so hungry that he eats his own shoes, and pronounces them tasty; and the story of a woman who watches her own husband die on the doorstep. Both funny and tragic this collection recreate the cataclysmic events of our Revolution.

TIGER AT THE GATES
Christopher Fry, trans. from Jean Giraudoux   tragedy
15m 7f   SF
Staged with a bare set except for two large gates and a stalking tiger, this play opens with the arrival of Hector, straight from battle, who tries to convince

Ulysses of the insanity of the Trojan War. In spite of their agreement, however, the poets need their muse, the kings need their customs, and so, in spite of the warriors' logic, the war goes on.

TIME OUT FOR GINGER

Ronald Alexander   **comedy**

5m 5f   **DPS**

A humorous and very human play about a banker who spices up his life by lecturing on self-fulfillment at the local high school. He realizes that he may have gone too far, however, when his own daughter takes his lectures to heart and tries out for the football team. The hilarious repercussions include the father's job being jeopardized, the other daughters' suffering social lives, and Ginger's own boyfriend expressing disapproval. All ends well, of course, as the play's final scene has the whole family venturing out to see one of the other daughters in a play.

'TIS PITY SHE'S A WHORE

Ford   **tragedy**

mix   **public domain**

The play centers on a young girl who has an incestuous love affair with her own brother and in the process rejects a number of highly eligible suitors. Among them is a wealthy nobleman who is the most persistent and whom she is finally forced to marry.

TO BE YOUNG, GIFTED, AND BLACK

Lorraine Hansberry   **biography**

2m 4f   **SF**

Adapted from Lorraine Hansberry's own work about her life, *To Be Young ,Gifted, and Black* is kaleidoscope of images and scenes about this talented and famous Black artist. The play includes scenes from her plays, diaries, poems, and personal memories to highlight the experiences that shaped her life. An extraordinary collection that lends powerful insight into the American Black experience.

TO BURN A WITCH

James L. Bray   **one-act drama**
4f   **Dramatic**

In a bare cell in Salem, Massachusetts, two terrified young women await their trial. Mary and Ruth have long been close friends and they are now both on trial for witchcraft. While Mary refuses to lie, even to save her own life, Ruth chooses to "confess." Confused by the conflicting stories of the two close friends, the questioners remain dissatisfied. Finally, Ruth fakes a seizure and implicates Mary. Mary must now choose and in the last powerful scene, she does.

TO GILLIAN ON HER 37TH BIRTHDAY

Brady   **play**
2m 5f   **Broadway**

Contemporary drama that examines the function and the nature of one man's ongoing process of mourning the death of his young wife Gillian. David, the main character, has come to terms with his grief by establishing a continuing, albeit phantom, relationship with his deceased spouse. Although comfortable and competent with his personal solution to her death and his life without her, he's forced to deal with his friends and relatives in the real world. They fear that his "solution" will be his own personal undoing.

TO KILL A MOCKINGBIRD

Lee & Sergel   **drama**
11m 6f   **Dramatic**

Also available in a one-act version, *To Kill a Mockingbird* is an adaptation of Harper Lee's novel about a young girl growing up in a rural Southern town. Set in 1935, the play follows Scout, her brother Jem, their father Atticus, and Calpurnia, their housemaid and mother-figure. The action revolves around Atticus's decision to defend a young Black man accused of a grave crime. As friends become enemies and enemies friends, Scout begins to grow and understand the world around her. A truly thought-provoking play.

TODAY I AM A FOUNTAIN PEN

Israel Horovitz   **drama**

5m 3f   **DPS**

The first in a trilogy of plays based on the stories by Morley Torgov. At only ten years of age, Irving Yanover is a piano prodigy who aggravates his parents with his fondness for bacon. Although young Irving knows that they eat it too, he can only wonder at their duplicity. A subplot is the plight of Annie, the Ukrainian house-keeper whose parents oppose her romance with a young Italian. All of these conflicts are resolved with humor and love in this warm play for audiences of all faiths.

TOM SAWYER

Paul Kester   **comedy**

13m 8f   **SF**

A play based on the famous book by Samuel Clemens or, perhaps more appropriately, Mark Twain. In a carefully condensed version, this play brings all of the adventures and beloved characters of the novel to life. An epic of American boyhood that all audiences will welcome.

TONIGHT AT 8:30

Noel Coward   **nine one-acts**

variable   **SF**

A clever group of nine one-act plays that can be presented in three nights of savvy theater or grouped to reflect the needs of the individual group. Plays include *Ways and Means,* about an heiress and her gambling husband; *We Were Dancing* about a married woman who falls in love while dancing only to realize she doesn't mean it; and *Still Life* about the brief romance between a doctor and his patient.

TREASURE ISLAND

Timothy Mason   **short play**

21m 4f   **ICM**

Adapted from Robert Louis Stevenson's novel, this play is a fast-paced pirate tale full of intrigue and treasure. A young boy finds a secret treasure map in the sea-chest of a crying man. A rough and tumble group of men come together to seek out the treasure, bringing the boy along. On board there is mutiny and fighting, danger and adventure. The boy, Jim Hawkins, becomes a hero when he saves the ship, rescues the treasure, and outwits the pirates.

TRI ZLATE VLASY DEDA VSEVEDA (THE 3 GOLDEN HAIRS OF GRANDFATHER KNOW IT ALL)

Pamela Gerke   one-act

min / max 30 m&f   S&K

This is a tale of changing fortunes and fate. A king who likes to hunt wild animals is stuck in the woods the night his wife is giving birth to their daughter. That night in the woods, a boy is born, and the King overhears the fates prophesy that the common-born boy will marry his daughter. His attempts to keep the boy from succeeding, resulting in his own fall from fortune to the ferryman.

TRIBUTE

Bernard Slade   drama/comedy

3m 4f   SF

The main character in this play is Scottie Templeton, a charming but entirely irresponsible agent and former scriptwriter who is everyone's friend and quite the ladies' man. Although he has never taken anything in life seriously, even marriage and fatherhood, Scottie is suddenly faced with the tragic fact of his own imminent death. When his neglected son comes to visit, Scottie desperately tries to make peace. Finally, the two are dramatically reconciled as the son convinces Scottie to pursue treatment.

TRIXIE TRUE, TEEN DETECTIVE

Kelly Hamilton   musical

4m 4f   SF

Trixie's author, Joe Sneed, has been commissioned by his boss, Miss Sneed, to write yet another story about the unbelievably clever young crimefighter. Tired of Trixie, Joe conceives of one last mystery in which Trixie will meet her maker. Fortunately, Joe realizes that if he wants to keep his job and his chances of a romance with Miss Sneed, the ever-popular Trixie must survive and so he quickly devises a way for the young detective to save herself and solve the mystery.

TWAIN BY THE TALE
Dennis Snee   **monologues**
2m 3f   **SF**

An evening of Mark Twain's legendary wit, *Twain by the Tale* is a collection of monologues and sketches that brings together some of the delightful perceptions of one of America's favorite storytellers. Included are favorite targets such as bigots, politicians, moralists, and monarchs as well as Twain's timeless insight into friendship, good breeding, and vice.

TWELFTH NIGHT
William Shakespeare   **comdy**
11m 3f   **public domain**

This play is a comedy containing all of the classic elements of disguise, twins mistaken for twins, and misdirected affections. Viola, disguised as a boy, is the central figure. She has fallen in love with a duke, who has fallen in love with a woman whom he sends Viola to woo. When the woman falls in love with Viola, in her boyish disguise, matters become even more complex. The situation is resolved, eventually, with the arrival of Viola's twin brother Sebastian.

TWELVE ANGRY MEN (WOMEN)
Reginald Rose & Sherman L. Sergel   **drama**
12m (f)   **Dramatic**

The setting is a courtroom where a nineteen-year-old boy has just stood trial for the fatal stabbing of his own father. At first an open-and-shut case, one of the jurors begins to open the others' eyes and suggests that it might not be such a clear case of guilt. As tempers rise and the murder is re-examined and re-enacted, the characters of the jurors themselves are revealed in this turbulent and electrifying piece.

TWO FOR THE ROAD
Carla Schlarb   **one-act drama**
3m 4f   **SF**

A haunting play that begins with start of a school day, Mrs. Harris's class appears to be like every other class until a boy and a girl enter. The two tardy students are ignored by the other students. At first they believe it is per the instructions of their teacher, but after discussing the previous night's date, the two teens realize that they are actually ghosts. They have died in a drunk-driving accident, two more victims of the tragic trend of teenage alcoholism.

TWO GENTLEMEN OF VERONA
William Shakespeare   **romance**
11m 3f   **public domain**

This is a comedy with a somewhat darker taint. Proteus betrays both his lover, Julia, and his best friend Valentine, when he falls in love with Valentine's lover. Upon being discovered, he readily apologizes, falls back in love with Julia, and everyone appears prepared to live happily ever after.

TWO NOBLE KINSMEN
William Shakespeare/ Fletcher   **romance**
13m 7f   **public domain**

This is the most well-known play of John Fletcher (a contemporary of Shakespeare). Based on characters from Greek mythology and a plot originating in the *Decameron* by Boccaccio and Chaucer's *Canterbury Tales*. Fletcher embellishes and complicates the story line with subplots and intentional pathos. Characters include "The Two Noble Kinsmen" Palamon, Arcite, Hippolyta Queen of the Amazons, Theseus King of Athens, and Emilia Hippolyta's sister.

U

UFO!

Thomas F. Monteleone   comedy
8m 2f   WM

A college student unwittingly involves himself in the strange world of self-styled investigators of the UFO phenomenon. When Vincent Manzara calls a radio station talk show to make fun of a guest who claims to have been abducted by a flying saucer, complications ensue. By claiming to have been abducted by the same aliens, he causes a sensation in the UFO community of true believers. He is interviewed and assailed by a variety of "investigators"—each one more bizzare and tragically comic than the last. Eventually, Vincent is not certain whether or not his claimed experience was real or imagined and he learns a valuable lesson by play's end.

UNCLE TOM'S CABIN

George L. Aiken   drama
15m 6f   SF

Adapted from Harriet Beecher Stowe's famous novel of the same name, *Uncle Tom's Cabin* is a six-act play that captures all of the horror and sentimentality of Stowe's history-making novel about slavery in nineteenth-century America. Uncle Tom, George, little Eva, Cassie, and all of the beloved and despised characters of the original appear in this nearly epic play that has been performed thousands of times by theater groups throughout the country.

UNCLE VANYA

Anton Chekhov   comic drama
5m 4f   SF

Chekhov's comic drama about a man and his frustrated passion for a young lady who is married to an old and sick man. The young woman, and the young miss of the house, are both in love with the doctor who attends the dying old man. The play follows these romantic entanglements for one season in the Russian countryside. A truly Chekhovian play complete with deeply human characters.

UP THE DOWN STAIRCASE

Christopher Sergel from Bel Kaufman   **comedy**

12m 18f   **Dramatic**

A simple set allows this play to capture a sense of the entire school in which this moving play takes place. It is the story of a young, attractive teacher who arrives at her new job only to find herself quickly entangled in a romance, disagreements with the administrator, and most of all, with the sometimes heartbreaking problems of the students whom she comes to care so much about.

UTTER GLORY OF MORRISSEY HALL

Clark Gesner & Nagle Jackson   **musical**

4m 18f   **SF**

A whimsical and lighthearted look into the mischievous lives of a group of young girls living in an English boarding school. The play takes the form of chronicling a series of harmless but nutty pranks carried out by the students of Morrissey Hall. Throughout the play is the irrepressibly optimistic character of the headmistress who tries to maintain a center of sanity amidst the zany but benign hijinks of the girls.

V

VALENTIN AND VALENTINA

Mikhail Roachin trans. by Hastings & IVacchina drama
8m 10f Dramatic

A variation on the Romeo and Juliet theme, this story of two young lovers takes place in Russia. Valentin and Valentina are passionately in love, but both of their families disapprove because of the class difference between them. When both families become obsessed with the work principle, all attention is focused on Valentin's career and further pressure is put on their relationship when it threatens the advance of his work. At the center of this play, of course, is love and what the characters think about it.

VALENTINE'S DAY

Horton Foote drama
6m 4f DPS

Part of Horton Foote's nine-play cycle about the Robedaux family in Harrison, Texas. Set in the 1917, this play focuses on one young couple during the time of World War I. Horace Robedaux and Elizabeth Vaughn have married in spite of their parents' objections. The heart of the action comes from the daily lives of these two young people and their friends and neighbors, all of whom are keeping secrets from each other. The couple is awaiting the birth of their firstborn, and the play ends with a hopeful look into the future.

VASILISA PREKRASNAIA (VASILISA THE BEAUTIFUL)

Pamela Gerke one-act
min 9 / max 25 m&f S&K

This Russian tale is a combination of *Cinderella* and *Rumplestilkin*. Vasilisa's evil stepmother does everything she can to get rid of the little girl. Vasilisa is protected by the kookla—magic doll—her mother gave her. After her stepmother sends her out into the woods for a light, she is captured by a witch. Vasilisa's doll helps her perform all the impossible demands the witch makes, and she is finally released with a magic light that takes care of her stepsisters and stepmother, and even wins her the Czar.

THE VIGIL

Ladislas Fodor   biblical

18m 6f   SF

The Vigil is the dramatic retelling of the Easter story in a modern setting. The time is the days between Good Friday and Easter Sunday; in a small-town American courtroom, a man known simply as the Gardener is charged with moving Christ's body after the crucifixion. The trial proceeds with each character revealing what he or she saw that day, and it comes to an electrifying end as Mary Magdalene reenacts her meeting with Jesus in the Garden.

VILLEGGIATURA: A TRILOGY

Goldoni, tr. R. Cornthwaite   comedy

8m 3f   S&K

Villeggiatura: A Trilogy is a long play about love, lost love, and love gone astray. Yuppiedom in eighteenth-century Italy. In these three plays, two determined young ladies vie for the latest fashion in gowns, marriage, and the attention of a seductive young man. Great translation for young actors!

THE VIRGIN OF ORLEANS

Friedrich von Schiller, trans. by Johanna Setzer   romantic tragedy

20m 6f   SF

A translation of an unorthodox version of the life of Joan of Arc. Written long before her canonization, this version includes palace intrigue, Joan's guilty infatuation with an English general, and her glorious death on the battlefield as she leads the French army to victory.

A VOICE OF MY OWN

Elinor Jones   drama

min. 5f   DPS

A Voice of My Own chronicles the literary achievement of women through the cleverly interwoven words and works of twenty-four outstanding women writers. Spanning a breathtaking twenty-six centuries, it follows not only the achievements but the disappointments and hardships endured by these brilliant women.

Forced to hide behind male names and anonymity, they persevered to have their voices heard. A tribute to women writers and to "the other half" of humanity.

VOICES FROM THE HIGH SCHOOL
Peter Dee   **comedy/drama**
flexible   **SF**

A series of scenes and monologues written specifically for high school students looking to perform material that relates directly to their own lives. The vignettes depict the pain and humor of growing up fast and furiously. Themes include love, sex, drugs, the student-teacher relationship, suicide, and more. A cuttingly honest look at American teenagers.

VOICES FROM WASHINGTON HIGH
Craig Sodaro   **drama**
7m 8f   **Dramatic**

In a play that could have come straight from today's headlines, *Voices from Washington High* examines the violence of America's high school hallways. A group of seniors at Washington High look forward to the best year ever, but the arrival of a new student pits one against the other in an explosive and tragic ending. Strong characters include Jessy, the smartest student in the class; Coulee Mark, the new kid; and the guidance counselor who tries to warn them. The voices of the students, the teachers, their friends and families, come alive in this powerful play.

W

WAIT UNTIL DARK

Frederick Knott   mystery

6m 2f   DPS

The central character in this chilling tale is a young blind girl, a clever and enterprising woman not to be pitied but rather admired for her skill and ingenuity in dealing with the scoundrels in the play. The young woman's husband has gone away on assignment. Left alone, she soon discovers mysterious intruders who seem to have killed someone. Aided only by her own wits and the help of a prying little girl who lives upstairs, the young wife manages to survive and uncover the shocking mystery.

WATERWORKS

E. J. Safirstein   one-act comic drama

1m 3f   SF

A gentle and funny play, *Waterworks* is a one-act that tells the story of two teenagers who are forced to confront the reality of death and illness. Ruth is brash and aggressive while Ben is more quiet and studious; the conflict that arises between these two young people is the source of humor in this play and eventually becomes the basis of a friendship that will help them both through their grief.

WAY DEEP

Katherine Burger   one-act drama

3m 2f   SF

A play perfect for high schools, it involves two young lovers who, discouraged by their parents, run away from their homes. The play follows them through the processes of coping with the loss of their families' support, trying to find jobs, and live in a world that is unlike anything they imagined. The play focuses on not only the young people but the distraught parents as well; it ends with their capitulation in a stunning recognition scene.

WEST SIDE STORY
Laurents and Sondheim musical
27m 9f & chorus RH

The time-honored American theater classic, West Side Story is a modern-day variation on the Romeo and Juliet theme, only this time the setting is the West Side streets of New York City and the form is a musical play. Once again, love is the central theme as two young people confront their families' cultural prejudices and the pressures of their streetwise peers in the hope of living happily together.

WHADDA 'BOUT MY LEGAL RIGHTS
Marshall & Andrew Lauren Goldman Duxbury musical
3m 3f SF
A clever musical that is a great way to educate high school students about the American legal system. The play follows six teenagers as they confront a variety of legal issues that include: racism and sexism, dress codes, abuse, child support, and teen pregnancy. A meaningful but fun way to address real concerns of today's teens.

WHAT DID WE DO WRONG?
Henry Denker comedy
5m 3f SF
A consistently funny comedy about a father dealing with his son's turn to the protest genre. *What Did We Do Wrong?* is the question that one father must ask when his son is expelled for handcuffing himself to the dean. When the son shows up with his hippie friends, the father decides to join them in an effort to make the young radicals realize exactly what they are doing.

WHAT I DID LAST SUMMER
A. R. Gurney play
2m 4f DPS
Set during the end of the Second World War in a well-to-do vacation colony, *What I Did Last Summer* is the story of Charlie, a rebellious fourteen-year-old boy who is spending the summer with his mother and sister before going to boarding

school in the fall. With his father off fighting in the Pacific, Charlie intended to spend the summer loafing with his friends, but his need for money forces him to take a job as a handyman for an art teacher. The teacher opens Charlie's mind to a world of painting and sculpture that ultimately results in a conflict between him and his mother, a conflict that raises as many questions as it answers and that will shape the rest of Charlie's life.

WHEN PEOPLE COULD FLY
L.E. McCullough   one-act
6m 7f   S&K
A play that illuminates a fascinating, little-known African-American folktale from the antebellum South. Although it depends on elements of the fantastic in its employment of magic, it also uses the institution of slavery as a frame for its theme of enduring the unendurable. Inspiring and challenging, and full of music.

WHEN THEY SPEAK OF RITA
Daisy Foote   drama
3m 2f   Paradigm
Rita Potter is trapped in a dull existence in rural New Hampshire. To make up for her seeming failure, Rita pushes her son and his girlfriend to reach for more than she did. When her efforts are all met with resistance, Rita makes drastic changes in her life, changes that prove disasterous. Daisy Foote offers a story where the young people are more capable than the adults to boldly face the world with responsibility.

WHISPERINGS IN THE GRASS
Suzanne Granfield   drama
5m 1f, guitarist   SF
In a style similar to *Spoon River Anthology*, *Whisperings in the Grass* explores the longing that drove people toward the West in the 1800s. Leaving their secure Eastern homes, thousands of Americans embarked on a historical journey to start a new life in an unknown land; they searched for freedom and an open road in a land that seemed boundless. A searching and beautiful play.

THE WHITE HOUSE
A. E. Hotchner history
7m 3f SF

Impressive vignettes set in the White House, this play follows the American Presidents and the first families from Washington to Wilson, with many in-between. A maid acts as the interlocutor in this close look at the personal tragedies, trials, and triumphs of the wives and families of some of America's most famous men. Including letters and writings from the historical events and memories of the people themselves, this is a unique look at American history.

WHO IS CHASING WHOM!
Lynne Alvarez one-act
2m or 2f JKA

Who Is Chasing Whom!, a short, original play by Lynne Alvarez, contains five sequences of mostly silent acting. The two characters are Who, a dreamer whose sense of reality is quite different from others' and Whom, a free spirit with a practical sense of the world. Variations in casting can dramatically affect the overall sense of this distinct and thought-provoking play. A fun challenge for young actors.

WHO WILL CARRY THE WORD
Delbo play
23f Agent

A dramatic documentary of playwright Charlotte Delbo's two-year experience in a German concentration camp. Her story involves a group of women and the psychological and physical tortures they endured. Bleak, raw, and brutally realistic, the play succeeds upon its brilliant evocations and provocative dialogue.

WHODUNNIT
Shaffer & Anthony mystery/comedy
7m 3f SF

Whodunit is a one-act mystery-farce. Walter Beardsley brings his new wife home; there she meets Carey Fielding, whom she introduces as a close friend of her first husband. The Sheriff soon receives as call from Walter saying his life has been threatened and then Walter disappears. But that is only the beginning of this wild mystery that will have audiences guessing until the last scene.

WHO'S CRAZY NOW?

Gerald Bell   **farce**

3m 9f   **SF**

Set in an insane asylum, *Who's Crazy Now?* features schoolteachers who have gone mad trying to educate their students. The women in the beginning of this farce talk and act like their former charges in a hilarious start to the play. A romance is introduced between the niece of the superintendent and a young doctor. At first both think the other is an inmate. Finally, when the young woman realizes what has happened to the teachers, she decides to marry the doctor, giving up her ambition to be a teacher.

WHOSE LIFE IS IT ANYWAY?

Brian Clark   **drama**

9m 5f   **Dramatic**

A brilliant play about a battle of the wits between a man paralyzed in a car accident and the doctor who is determined to keep him alive. Ken Harrison was a successful sculptor until his accident, and although he is outwardly cheerful, he does not want to live as a medical achievement. The doctor, a brilliant man, wants to keep him alive regardless of quality of life. Finally Ken involves the Judge as the battle continues to decide whose life is it anyway?

WHY DO WE LAUGH?

Stephen Gregg   **drama**

4m 4f   **Dramatic**

When she is six years old, Merideth tells everyone that she hates her neighbor Andrew Powers. At sixteen, she tells Andrew the same thing but goes to the dance with him anyway. At forty-five, Merideth and Andy are married and have a great deal to share with one another. Even at sixty-six, Merideth continues to learn about and from her husband. A challenging play that is easily produced. All eight characters, the couple at each of the four stages of life, remain on stage at all times.

WILD OATS
James McLure comedy
23m 6f DPS
A comedy based on a famous Restoration play by John O'Keefe, *Wild Oats* is set in the wild and woolly West. The scene has been changed from English drawing rooms to Western saloons and prairies and the characters from servants and lustful gentry to music hall girls and cavalry men, but the freewheeling humor is the same. Themes include long-lost parents and children united, an evil business man, a hero who can stop a train with one hand, and a slippery preacher. All combine for a wild farce that actors will enjoy as much as audiences.

WINDSHOOK
Mary Gallagher drama
4m 3f H&CA
A stranger breezes into a small town, capturing the heart of the prettiest girl around. The play deals with dreams and compromising those dreams to be with the people we love. Strong supporting roles.

THE WIZ
William F. Brown & Charlie Smalls musical
11 various SF
A musical version of L. Frank Baum's beloved *The Wonderful Wizard of Oz*. A fantasy of rock, gospel, and soul music, Dorothy's adventures in the land of Oz come to life in an opulent dreamlike version of a well-known story. All of the favorite characters—the Scarecrow, the Tin Man, and the Cowardly Lion—are present in this fun and fantastical musical version.

WOMEN AND WALLACE
Jonathan Marc Sherman drama
1m 4f DPS
Women and Wallace is the story of a young man, Wallace, and his relationships with the women in his life. The play begins when the handsome man is eighteen but quickly flashes back to him as a six-year-old who discovers his mother's body

after she commits suicide. This grizzly discovery will haunt him throughout his life and greatly affect his relationships with women. In the kaleidoscopic scenes that follow, Wallace continues his journey toward manhood.

THE WOODMAN AND THE GOBLINS
Don Nigro   **one-act dark comedy**
1m 3f   SF
A dark comedy simply set with a bare stage and four wooden chairs. A lonely woodcutter has found three eggs in the middle of a dark forest. He brings them home and watches them hatch into three beautiful girls who at first enchant him, then torment him, and finally destroy the helpless Woodman. Hauntingly dark and humorous, this play is based on an old European folktale beloved by Charles Dickens.

THE WOOLGATHERER
William Mastrosimone   **drama/love story**
1m 1f   SF
The two characters are Rose, a shy and rather creepy five-and-dime salesgirl, and Cliff, a hardworking, hard-drinking truck driver. The witty and brash Cliff has picked up Rose and been invited back to her room in a dreary Philadelphia apartment building. Both characters are starved for love, one an innocent dreamer, the other a rough and hardened working man.

Y

YOU CAN'T TAKE IT WITH YOU
Moss Hart & George S. Kaufman   **comedy**
9m 7f   **DPS**

The story of two families: the Sycamores who, if mad, reveal that the rest of the world is even madder; and the Kirbys who aren't quite ready for the happy madness of the Sycamores. Tony, the attractive young Kirby, is in love with Alice Sycamore; only his perseverance manages to overcome his family's dislike of his intended's family. Eventually his father is won over by the zany family, particularly the ex-Grand Duchess. A popular comedy that has found success everywhere.

YOU'RE A GOOD MAN CHARLIE BROWN
Gordon & Gesner   **musical**
4m 2f   **TW**

Based on the comic strip, *Peanuts,* this charming musical contains Charles M. Schulz's most lovable characters: Charlie Brown and his sister Lucy, Linus, Peppermint Patty, Marcy, and the rest of the Peanuts' gang. Songs include: the title song, "Snoopy," "Kite," "Dr. Lucy," "The Red Baron," and more.

YOU'RE LIVE WITH BIG-FOOT WALLACE!
L.E. McCullough   **one-act**
7m 7f   **S&K**

An inventive original play that poses an interesting question: What happens to figures from American folklore when their stories are no longer being told? In this story, a handful of characters, including John Henry, Joe Magarac, and Big-Foot Wallace, appear in the present to interact on television with an "action-news" reporter.

THE YOUNG AND FAIR

N. Richard Nash   **drama**

21f   **DPS**

Set in a fashionable junior college for women, *The Young and the Fair* is about the fight for honesty and truth. The Director of the college finds that a student has accused two other students of wrongdoing, but both are innocent and are being blackmailed by a twisted and jealous girl. A alumna and her idealistic younger sister—an entering student—help the Director and eventually see justice through to the end. A dramatic play about idealism and personal ethics that is perfect for a large female cast.

Z

THE ZOMBIE
Tim Kelly   **thriller**

4m 4f   **SF**

A comedy-thriller set in a Florida swamp, *The Zombie* takes place in the decaying mansion of Baron Samedi. There, using the ancient art of voodoo, he and the crooked sheriff turn criminals and illegal immigrants into zombies that are then hired out as laborers. A young man and his two female intruders stumble onto the terrifying production. A humorous and chilling play that is fun and easy to produce.

Key to Leasing Agents

Playwrights sometimes change representatives or agencies, therefore, it may be necessary to consult the Dramatist Guild of America, the internet, or your local library.

The majority of agents and agencies are located in New York.

Anchorage Press
Post Office Box 8067
New Orleans, LA 70182
Tel 504-283-8868
fax 504-866-0502

Author's League of America
330 West 42nd Street
New York, NY 10036
Tel 212-564-8350

[Baker's] Plays
PO Box 699222
Quincy, MA 02269-9222
Tel 617-745-0805
fax 617-745-9891
www.Bakersplays.com

Bantam
Division of Doubleday Dell Pub
1540 Broadway
New York, NY 10036
Tel 212-354-6500

Bret Adams Limited
448 West 44th St
New York, NY 10036
Tel 212-765-5630
fax 212-265-2212

[Broadway] Play Publishers
56 E. 81
New York, NY 10028-0202
Tel 212-772-8334
fax 212-772-8358
E-mail: Broadwaypl@aol.com

[CTC] California Theatre Center
Po Box 2007
Sunnyvale, CA 94087
Tel 408-245-2978

[Dramatic] Publishing Co.
311 Washington Street
PO Box 129
Woodstock, IL 60098
Tel 815-338-7170
fax 800-334-5302

Dramatics
3368 Central Parkway
Cincinnati, OH 45225-2392
Tel 513-559-1996

Dramatist Guild of America
1501 Broadway, Suite 701
New York, NY 10036
Tel 212-398-9366
fax 212-944-0420

[DPS] Dramatists Play Service
440 Park Avenue South
New York NY 10016
Tel 212-683-8960
fax 212-213-1539
E-mail: Postmaster@dramatists.com

The [Gersh] Agency
130 West 42nd Street
New York, NY 10036

[GA] Grove Atlantic
841 Broadway
New York, NY 10003
Tel 212-614-7850
fax 212-614-7886

[H&CA] Harden & Curtis Assocites
850 7th Avenue
Suite 405
New York, NY 10019
Tel 212-977-8502

[H&W] Hill and Wang
Div. of Farrar, Strauss & Giroux Inc.
19 Union Square W.
New York, NY 10003
Tel 212-741-6900

[ICM] International Creative Management
40 West 57th Street
New York, NY 10019
Tel 212-556-5600
fax 212-556-5665

Johns Hopkins
2715 North Charles St
Baltimore, MD 21218
Tel 410-516-6968

[JKA] Joyce Ketay Agency
1501 Broadway
Suite 1910
New York, NY 10036
Tel 212-354-6825
fax 212-354-6732

Knopf
201 East 50th St
New York, NY 10022
Tel 212-751-2600
fax 212-572-8700

[MT1] Music Theatre International
545 8th Ave
New York, NY 10019
Tel 212-868-6668
fax 212-643-8465

Paradigm
10100 Santa Monica Blvd, 25th Floor
Los Angeles, CA 90067

Public—Public Domain—These
plays are available without fee.

[RH] Random House
201 East 50th Street
New York, NY 10022
Tel 212-751-2600
fax 212-572-8700

[RHML]
Rogers & Hammerstein
229 West 28th St
11th Floor
New York, NY 10001
Tel 212-564-4000

[RSHM] Riverside Sh. H. Mifflin
Sub of Houghton Mifflin Co.
425 Spring Lake Drive
Utasca, Uk 60143
Tel 800-656-8420

[SF] Samuel French
45 West 25th Street
New York, NY 10010-2751
Tel 212-206-8990
fax 212-206-1429

[S&K] Smith & Kraus Publishers
PO Box 127
Lyme, NH 03768
Tel 603-643-6431
fax 603-643-1831

[SSA] Susan Schulman Lit. Agency
454 W. 44 St
New York, NY 10036
Tel 212-713-1633
fax 212-581-8830

[TW] Tams-Witmark Music Library
560 Lexington Avenue
New York, NY 10022
Tel 212-688-2525
fax 212-688-3232

[TMax] Theater Maximus
1650 Broadway
New York, NY 10019
Tel 212-765-5913

[U of C] University of Chicago Press
5801 Ellis Avenue
Chicago, IL 60637
Tel 773-702-7700
fax 773-702-9756

[WM] William Morris Agency
1325 Avenue of the Americas
New York, NY 10019-6011
Tel 212-586-5100